Networking Like A Pro is the most comprehensive book I've seen on
networking—bar none. From beginning to end, Misner and Hilliard
divulge networking concepts and strategies which will catapult
you from an average networker to a master networker and
empower you to achieve greatness in business and life.

—Jack Canfield, co-author of *Chicken Soup for the Soul*
and *The Success Principles*

Wow! This book breaks the mold in professional networking.
Its practical, powerful ideas will accelerate your success
in ways you cannot imagine.

—Brian Tracy, chairman and CEO of Brian Tracy International and author
of *Million Dollar Habits*

Done well, effective networking is 'the speed of trust' in action.
No one understands networking like Ivan Misner, so if you want to
get the maximum results possible from your networking
efforts, you need to read this book—period.

—Stephen M. R. Covey, author of *The New York Times* and number-one
Wall Street Journal bestseller *The Speed of Trust*

Dr. Ivan Misner is to networking what Michelangelo is to the Sistine Chapel. So, absolutely everything you've ever wanted to know about networking is guaranteed to be discussed in Dr. Misner's new book, *Networking Like a Pro*. Save yourself a lifetime of networking trial and error; read this book!

—DR. TONY ALESSANDRA, AUTHOR OF *THE PLATINUM RULE* AND HALL-OF-FAME KEYNOTE SPEAKER

The title says it all and this book surely does not disappoint. But don't take my word for it; read *Networking Like a Pro*, apply the new knowledge you gain to your networking efforts, and the results you get will speak volumes.

—MICHAEL E. GERBER, AUTHOR OF *BEYOND THE E-MYTH*

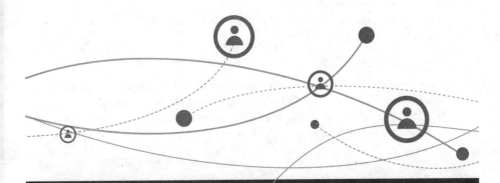

NETW●RKING LIKE A PRO

SECOND EDITION

TURNING CONTACTS INTO CONNECTIONS

IVAN MISNER, PH.D.
NEW YORK TIMES BESTSELLING AUTHOR & FOUNDER OF BNI
AND BRIAN HILLIARD

EP
Entrepreneur
PRESS®

Publisher: Entrepreneur Press
Cover Design: Andrew Welyczko
Production and Composition: Eliot House Productions

This publication is designed to provide accurate and authoritative information
in regard to the subject matter covered. It is sold with the understanding that
the publisher is not engaged in rendering legal, accounting, or other professional
services. If legal advice or other expert assistance is required, the services of a
competent professional person should be sought.

Givers Gain® and VCP Process® are registered trademarks of BNI. Certified
Networker® and Referrals for Life® are registered trademarks of the Referral
Institute. Networking Like a Pro!® is a registered trademark of Agito Consulting.

Library of Congress Cataloging-in-Publication Data
   Names: Misner, Ivan R., 1956– author. | Hilliard, Brian, author.
   Title: Networking like a pro: turning contacts into connections / Ivan
      Misner, Brian Hilliard.
   Description: Second Edition. | Irvine, California: Entrepreneur Press, 2017.
      | Revised edition of the authors' Networking like a pro, c2009.
   Identifiers: LCCN 2017027584| ISBN 978-159918-604-7 (paperback) |
      ISBN 1-59918-604-7 (ebook)
   Subjects: LCSH: Business networks. | Business referrals. | BISAC:
      BUSINESS & ECONOMICS / Small Business. | BUSINESS
      & ECONOMICS / Skills. | BUSINESS & ECONOMICS /
      Entrepreneurship.
   Classification: LCC HD69.S8 M5724 2017 | DDC 650.1/3–dc23
   LC record available at https://lccn.loc.gov/2017027584

Printed in the United States of America

22 21 20 19 18   10 9 8 7 6 5 4 3 2 1

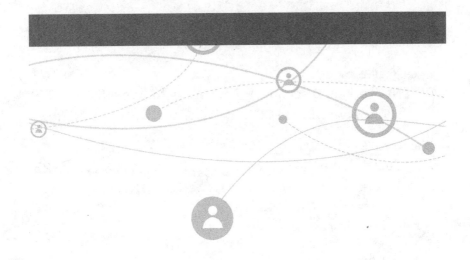

Contents

Acknowledgments xiii

INTRODUCTION
Debunking the Bunk 1
Debunking the Bunk 3
Wave of the Future 11

PART I
MINDSET

CHAPTER 1
Why Is Networking Not Taught in Schools? 15

CHAPTER 2

Networking Disconnect—Four Ways to Avoid It 19
The Great Disconnect. 20

CHAPTER 3

Social Capital 23
Back to the Future. 24
Outside the Cave 26
Relationships Are Currency. 27

CHAPTER 4

The Law of Reciprocity 29
It's the Law. 30
The Abundance Mindset 31

CHAPTER 5

Farming for Referrals 35
Drop the Gun, Grab the Plow. 36
Down on the Farm 39

CHAPTER 6

How Diverse Is Your Network? 41
Have a Diverse Network. 42
The Bottom Line 44

CHAPTER 7

The Butterfly Effect. 45

CHAPTER 8

Do Referrals Happen by Accident? 49

PART II

YOUR NETWORKING STRATEGY

CHAPTER 9

Your Network Should Be Both Wide and Deep 55

Make Contacts That Count. 56

Make It Personal. 56

The GAINS Profile. 58

CHAPTER 10

Building Quality Relationships Through the

VCP Process **61**

Visibility to Credibility to Profitability. 62

Be Patient. 64

CHAPTER 11

Where Networkers Gather **65**

Five Types of Business Networking Organizations. 65

Choosing the Networks That Are the Best for You 76

CHAPTER 12

Online Networking: Click Here to Connect. **79**

Looking Past the Hype. 80

Mind the Fundamentals. 81

Is Face-to-Face Communication Outmoded?. 81

Connecting with People at Web Speed. 82

Where Social and Face-to-Face Networking Meet. 87

Determining Your Online Networking Strategy 91

Other Ways to Communicate Online. 92

A Core Strategy That's Worth Knowing. 93

CHAPTER 13

Developing Your Target Market **95**

Spheres of Influence 96

PART III

NETWORKING FACE TO FACE

CHAPTER 14

Seven Characteristics of a Great Networker **103**

The Seven Characteristics That Make a
Great Networker 104

CHAPTER 15

The Five Least Important Skills to Be a
Great Networker **107**
What Matters Least 108

CHAPTER 16

Top Five Most Common Networking Mistakes **111**
Lack of Follow-Up 112
Unclear Unique Selling Proposition 112
Confusing Networking with Face-to-Face
Cold Calling 113
Not Responding Quickly to Referral Partners 114
Abusing the Relationship............................. 115
The Bottom Line 115

CHAPTER 17

Four Behavioral Styles to Know
When Networking **117**
Go-Getter... 118
Promoter 119
Nurturer.. 119
Examiner 120
The Bottom Line 121

CHAPTER 18

Where Do I Start? **123**

CHAPTER 19

The 12 x 12 x 12 Rule **129**
Look the Part Before Going to the Event (How Do
You Look from 12 Feet Away?)..................... 131

Make Sure Your Body Language Sends the Right Message
(How Do You Come Across from 12 Inches Away?) 131
Get Your Act Together 132
Have the First 12 Words Ready to Roll off Your Tongue
(What Are the First 12 Words out of Your Mouth?)..... 133

CHAPTER 20
**Three Questions to Determine the "Right"
Networking Event for You...................137**
Create Your Plan 138

CHAPTER 21
Where's Your Attention Focused? 145

CHAPTER 22
Standout Questions...........................149
Question Time 150
The Answers You Want 154

CHAPTER 23
Telling Your Company's Story...................155
Your Unique Selling Proposition....................... 156
Briefing Your Messenger 159
Getting Specific 161

CHAPTER 24
Quantity Is Fine, but Quality Is King..............163
It's All About the Relationships....................... 165
Maximize Your Event Strategy........................ 168

PART IV
MAKING YOUR NETWORK WORK

CHAPTER 25
**Getting More Referrals with a Formalized
Referral Strategy 173**

Write an Online Newsletter. 174
Create a Power Team of Complementary Businesses. 174
Consider a Client-Appreciation Event 175
Make Calls to Past Clients. 177
Include a P.S. in Your Email Signature 178
The Bottom Line 179

CHAPTER 26

**Keeping Your Social Capital Balance Sheet
in the Black** 181
Build Social Capital from Within 184

CHAPTER 27

Symptoms of a Referral 187
Top-of-Mind Problems. 188
The Trigger Point Approach. 190

CHAPTER 28

Gaining Their Confidence 191
Getting There 192
Staying for the Long Haul. 195

CHAPTER 29

Leveraging New Contacts. 197
Getting to the Next Stage 198

CHAPTER 30

The Power of Your Database 209
Choosing a CRM 212

CHAPTER 31

Becoming the Knowledgeable Expert 215

PART V

SECRETS OF THE MASTERS

CHAPTER 32

Becoming a Referral Gatekeeper 225

Guardian at the Gate 226

Hub of the Wheel...................................... 230

CHAPTER 33

Always Thank Your Referral Partners 233

Creative Rewards 234

CHAPTER 34

Networking at Non-Networking Events 243

Nontraditional Settings............................... 244

Ask, "How Can I Help?" 245

Be Sincere.. 247

Honor the Event...................................... 247

CHAPTER 35

Top Ten Ways Others Can Promote You 249

Systematic Referral Marketing......................... 250

CHAPTER 36

Five Levels of a Referral..................... 253

Level 1: Name and Contact Information 254

Level 2: Supplementary Material 255

Level 3: Share Experience............................. 255

Level 4: Introductory Call and/or Arrange a Meeting 255

Level 5: In-Person Introduction and Promotion 256

CHAPTER 37

The Networking Scorecard..................... 259

Send a Thank-You Card 260

Send a Thank-You Gift 261

Call a Referral Source 261

Arrange a One-to-One Meeting 261

Attend A Networking Event 261
Bring Someone with You to the Networking Event 261
Set Up an Activity with Multiple Referral Sources 262
Give a Referral 262
Share or Send an Article of Interest 262
Arrange a Group Activity for Clients 263
Nominate a Referral Source for Recognition 263
Display Another's Brochure in Your Office 263
Include Others in Your Newsletter 263
Arrange a Speaking Engagement 264
Post to Social Media 264
Share Something from Someone Else Via Social Media . . . 264
Invite a Source to Join Your Advisory Board 264

APPENDIX A

Credibility-Enhancing Materials Checklist 267
Checklist of Materials for Developing Your
    Word-of-Mouth Campaign 268

APPENDIX B

Do You Network Like a Pro? 271

About the Authors 273

Index. 277

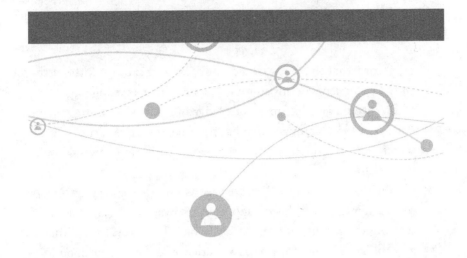

Acknowledgments

Writing a book is never easy, and doing it with another person is harder still. You have ideas to discuss, content to blend, and meetings to attend just to make sure you get it right. And with that said, we think we did just that . . . got it right.

Perfect? Probably not.

But "right" for the busy business professional looking to grow their business through referral marketing. We have many people to thank.

Heidi Scott Giusto and Jennifer Dorsey. An editor's job can unfortunately be a thankless one, and we would like to state, for the record, that this book would not be what it is today without the energy and talents of our editors—you all did an amazing job.

We would also like to acknowledge our publisher, Entrepreneur Press. They are a company that has proven to be a class-act operation through and through, and it's the reason we've done several books with them.

Finally, we saved the best for last as we owe the biggest thanks to our families who have supported us over the entire course of creating the second edition of this book. Thank you to the Misner and Hilliard families for your love, patience, and encouragement. We hope we make you proud.

Debunking
the Bunk

People sometimes ask us why we wrote this book, and the answer is simple: We wanted to give readers a blueprint on how to successfully build business through face-to-face networking. All too often, we run into business professionals who want to build a business by referrals, but for a variety of reasons, they come up short in their efforts.

Some have a unique selling proposition that isn't exactly right, and as a result, they aren't attracting their ideal clients. Others don't have an ideal client and are simply trying to be everything to everyone. And still others aren't sure where to network and are overwhelmed by all of their choices.

This book is for all of those folks and anyone else who wants to get more referrals from face-to-face networking.

Which brings us to another point: This book is NOT about social media marketing.

Is that a big part of what today's modern business professional is doing and should be doing? Absolutely. But is it the main focus of this book? No. There are tons of resources devoted to social media marketing, and, in an eye toward simplicity, we kept our focus on face-to-face networking (although we do briefly address social media).

We hope that while reading this resource you do two things:

Number 1: Select two or three ideas that you like and implement them within the next three days. All too often, we see people read books, listen to presentations, and then do nothing!

We want this book to inspire action. One of the topics we discuss regularly is if you want to get more, you have to be more first. This means that if you want to get more business and get more clients, then you have to be the type of business that attracts those people.

This means you have to be a good networker. You need to be a "connector" and offer valuable resources to others. You must be the type of person who others know, like, and trust. But you can't be any of these things if you fail to act, so read, learn, and then implement a few of our suggestions quickly. You won't regret that you did.

Number 2: Hold onto this book, and reference it throughout the years. Call us old-fashioned, but in today's digital age where everything is online, we hope this book stays in your physical library as a reference tool for years to come.

So, that's it.

We hope you enjoy the material...we certainly enjoyed putting it together.

And most importantly, we hope it gives you the tools and resources to go out and network like a pro!

DEBUNKING THE BUNK

As business professionals, we can tell you from personal experience how effective referral networking has been in the success of our own businesses. After reading this book, you will understand how it works and how it can be effective in your own business, but let's start by addressing some of the myths and misconceptions that people hit us with from time to time.

"I tried networking. It didn't work.
What's different about this?"

It's a common misconception that simply attending a networking event will bring you new business right away. It won't. Neither will just reading this book; there's no silver bullet in these pages.

Networking is simple, but it's not easy. If it were easy, everyone would do it, and do it well. But not everyone does. That's because it's a skill, like cooking and golf and carpentry, that takes knowledge, practice, commitment, and effort to learn and apply consistently. You can't just go out to the golf course, buy a club and a ball, whack the ball around a bit, and think you've played a round of golf. Neither can you walk unprepared into a gathering of potential networking contacts and suddenly become a competent networker— no matter how gregarious and sociable you are or how many books on networking you've read.

Networking is about forming and nurturing mutually beneficial relationships, which brings you new connections with large numbers of people, some of whom will become good customers. Networking also puts you in touch with other resources, such as industry experts, accountants, and lawyers, who can help your business in other ways.

Over time, you will get new business and your operation will grow stronger and more profitable. Will it happen overnight? No, and your new customers probably won't be among the first 10 or even 100 people you talk to, either. New business will come from people your networking contacts refer to you. But first you have to form solid relationships with your fellow networkers.

Some people go to a chamber of commerce mixer, exchange a few business cards, and then say, "There. I've networked." Wrong. That's only the beginning. You have to attend a variety of events to broaden your networking base; follow up with new contacts and learn all you can about their businesses, their goals, and their lives; maintain close ties with established contacts; provide referrals, information, and other benefits to your fellow networkers; and generally cultivate these relationships and keep them strong and healthy. That's networking. Only after you've been at it for quite some time will you begin to see a return on your investment. But when it comes, the return is strong and durable.

"Aren't most networking groups just full of people like me who are trying to build up a new business?"

When you go to a presentation or a seminar on networking, you might get that impression because the people you meet are there to learn something new, and so they tend to be younger folks. But if you go to a regular networking event or join a networking organization, you'll soon see that many of the people there tend to be older, established businesspeople. In fact, in the typical business networking group, the members range in age from the 20s through the 60s. Based on a study done at St. Thomas University, almost two-thirds of them are 40 or over. There's a good reason for this. It's usually the seasoned pros who have long since recognized and learned to use the benefits of networking to bolster their business. Many have used networking throughout the life of their business and are fully aware of the competitive advantage it offers. Older networkers often serve as mentors for younger businesspeople, which can be an enormous advantage to someone who is new to the art and science of networking.

The best networking groups are the ones whose membership is diverse in many ways—that is they have both older and younger members, a good balance of men and women, a mixture of races and ethnicities that are representative of the community, and include a wide variety of professions and specialties. Such a group can offer you the best opportunity to get referrals from outside your immediate circle of acquaintances, which puts you on the fast track to expanding your business.

"What good is networking if you can't measure the results?"

If you're expecting to find a direct, immediate correlation between your networking activities and the dollars you harvest as a result, you're going to be sorely disappointed. It's not like cold calling, where you can check off 500 phone numbers and see that you talked to 50 people and closed 7 sales and that 493 of your calls were a huge waste of your time. It's not like sending out 1,000 mailers and getting just 3 of them back, which gives you a hard number (exactly 0.3 percent) but pretty wimpy results (exactly 0.3 percent). If your goal is immediate results, no matter how poor, these alternatives may be right up your alley. Mass advertising? Sure, it works, but even that traditional method can't tell you exactly how many customers came into your store as a result of the enormous sum of money you spent.

The returns you receive through networking are like the apples you pick from an orchard you started from a single seed. You don't expect anything the first year, or even the second or third. But in the fourth year, that tree will not only bear fruit but also spread the seeds that will ultimately become a whole grove of apple trees. With networking, the time scale is not that daunting; it may not take years to start seeing results, but it will probably take many months. You might get a few early referrals, but the real payoff in measurable business comes after you've stuck with it long enough to build a substantial referral network—that's when you'll find that you're getting referrals from people you never knew about, people who are connected to you only through several intermediaries, so many and from so many sources that you may not even know exactly how many are the result of your networking.

Although the full complexity of your network may not be apparent even to you, the results of a good referral networking system are measurable. Toward the end of this book, in Appendix B, you'll find our Networking Scorecard, a tool for keeping track of your networking efforts. No, this is not a direct measure of the sales you're getting, but as you become an experienced businessperson, you'll find that the information on networking says volumes about the condition of your network and its implications of your eventual sales and business volume.

Here's another way to measure your networking success: of the people you meet at a networking event, what percentage of them remember you 72 hours later? This is one measure of your visible identity, and it's only one factor, but a significant one, in determining how successfully you are networking. Networking is more than just meeting people, and it isn't about how many sales you get from the people you meet. It's about how well you are remembered by a new contact and whether you differentiated yourself from the other five people she or he met that day.

One of the most important metrics is the number of coffee connections (follow-up meetings) you have with your new contacts—at least, the ones you want to network with. A contact that you do not follow up with is a contact that will never become part of your network. There will be no business—no sales, no referrals, no meeting the powerful CEO he knows—unless you follow through.

You can measure the results, but you have to be tracking the right networking activities. Most big companies have their salespersons track the wrong activities, and then they can't understand why their networking efforts are not working. To get the results you expect, you've got to track the right efforts.

"If my customers are satisfied, they'll give me referrals. Why should I join a networking group?"

Yes, customers can be a good source of referrals. Immediately after an especially good experience at your business, a happy client may talk you up to a friend who needs the service you provide, but it often ends there. A customer who is merely satisfied is not likely to go out of her way to tell others about you. And here's the kicker: The White House of Consumer Affairs found that 90 percent or more of unhappy customers will not do business with the offending company again. Furthermore, each unhappy customer is likely to share his or her grievance with at least nine other people and 13 percent will tell more than 20 other people. Customer-based word-of-mouth can hurt you more than help you.

A networking partner, by contrast, is always on the lookout for good customers for your business, just as you are always looking for people to send to your networking partners. Your fellow networkers also know a lot about your business, the kind of customers you want, and are experts in marketing you by word of mouth—the most powerful kind of marketing that exists. This kind of referral generation lasts much longer and brings you a steady stream of high-quality business, the kind that doesn't turn around and go to your competitor as soon as he holds his next clearance sale. You can get more good referrals from one or two loyal networking sources than from all the customers who come through your doors—and the customers you get are the kind you'll want to keep.

"How do I network if I'm not a naturally outgoing person?"

Go ahead and breathe a sigh of relief because you don't have to become Mr. Public Speaker, person-about-town, to be a successful networker. Most businesspeople, given a little real-world experience, naturally develop a certain level of comfort in dealing with customers, vendors, and others in their day-to-day transactions. Even people who are not gregarious or outgoing can form meaningful relationships and communicate.

Over years of teaching people the art of networking, we've found many techniques that can make the process a whole lot easier—especially for those who consider themselves introverted. For example, volunteering to be an ambassador or visitor host for a local business networking event can be a great way to get involved without feeling out of place.

Think about it. When you have guests at your house or office, what do you do? You engage them, make them feel comfortable, perhaps offer them something to drink. What you don't do is stand by yourself in the corner thinking about how you hate meeting new people.

By serving as a visitor host at your local chamber event, you effectively become the host of the party. Try it! You'll find it much easier to meet and talk to new people.

IVAN

Recently, my wife and I were sitting at the table having dinner and talking when I made an offhand comment about being an extrovert. She gave me a look and said, "Honey, I hate to break it to you, but you're an introvert."

I smiled and said, "Yeah, right. I'm a public speaker, and I'm the founder of the world's largest networking organization. And you say I'm an introvert?"

She then proceeded to name all the ways in which I was an introvert, supporting her argument with real-life examples of my behavior. I still couldn't believe it, but we've been married for 20 years so I had a sneaking suspicion she might actually know me pretty well.

The next day, I did some research online and found a test I could take. The results were a shock: I was a "situational extrovert"! That meant I was somewhat of a loner, reserved around strangers, but very outgoing in the right context.

That's when it finally hit me, "Oh my god! I'm an introvert!" In 1985, I started a business networking organization called BNI (Business Network International). To this day, when I visit a BNI region, I ask the director to have someone walk me around and introduce me to members and visitors. I tell her that this is so I can connect with as many people as possible, but in reality, it's because I'm uncomfortable walking around alone and introducing myself. Oh my god, I'm an introvert!

I realized that the whole notion of acting like the host, not the guest, and volunteering to be the ambassador at a chamber event or the visitor host at a BNI group were not just activities I recommended to all those poor introverts out there, but they were also ways that I, myself, employed to move around more comfortably at networking events. Oh my god, I'm an introvert! Who would have thought? (Besides my lovely wife, that is.)

Now, more than ever, I truly believe that whether you are an introvert or an extrovert, you can be good at networking. There are strengths and weaknesses to both traits; by finding ways to enhance the strengths and minimize the weaknesses, anyone can be a great networker.

BRIAN

This one really hits home for me. If you've seen me on stage talking to a bunch of folks and having a good time, you might find it hard to believe that I'm not a naturally outgoing person. But it's the truth. As someone who talks about sales and networking, I had to learn these techniques to help me get more business.

I knew early on that if I wanted to build my business through referrals, I would need to get better at meeting new people. So I started reading books like *Guerilla Marketing* by Jay Conrad Levinson and *Solution Selling* by Michael Bosworth and others on marketing in general and sales in particular. I also listened to my mom who always preached the idea that you need to focus on who you want to be, rather than who you are, so I made it a point to be more talkative at various networking events since that's who I wanted to be. I watched other people at events who I wanted to emulate and picked up some pointers from them, and when you put that all together—here I am.

"Getting business by a person-to-person referral sounds like something that used to happen when my great-grandfather was selling horse-drawn buggies. Why should I waste my time on a marketing method that's generations out of date?"

Yes, networking has been around a long time. It used to be the way that most businesses operated. In a small community, where everybody knows everybody, people do business with the people they trust, and they recommend these businesses to their friends. Small-town professionals naturally tend to refer business to each other, too, usually to those who return the favor, but often simply on the basis of whose service will reflect best on the referrer. If you're a plumber and you refer a customer to a dentist you know, you don't want that customer complaining to you a week later about what a lousy dentist you sent him to.

Today, most people do business on a larger scale, over a broader customer base and geographic area. More people now live in cities, and in even a small city most people are total strangers to one another. The personal connections of the old-style community, and the trust that went with them, are mostly gone. That's why a system for generating referrals among a group of professionals who trust one another is so important these days, and it is why referral networking is not only the way of the past but also the wave of the future. It's a cost-effective strategy with a long-term payoff. It's where business marketing is going, and it's where you need to go if you're going to stay in the game. As the great hockey player Wayne Gretzky said, "I don't skate to where the puck is, but where it's going to be."

"Networking is not a hard science."

WAVE OF THE FUTURE

Think about the most successful people you know. What do they have in common? Probably this: They have built a network of contacts that provide support, information, and business referrals. They have mastered the art and science of networking, and business flows their way almost as a matter of course.

It has taken these successful networkers years of hard work and perseverance to build their networks. It will take a similar commitment from you, too, but it won't take you as long, because you'll have one great advantage over the others: you'll have this book.

In these pages, we will show you how to develop and use a referral network as a long-term, sustainable business client-acquisition strategy, employing the tactics that have been found most effective by the pros. You will learn of many tools and techniques that will make it easier for you to build profitable relationships. You'll learn them faster than those who have gone before you and had to learn them by trial and error. Using this marketing strategy, you will be able to maintain a high-profit margin while providing better service to your clients, a combination that will put you far ahead of your competition.

Networking is the mainstream business development technique of the future. Businesspeople who invest in themselves by learning how to network like a pro will be rewarded with a long-term sustainable and profitable business.

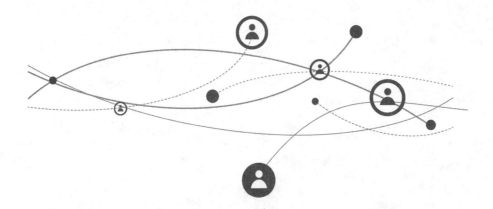

PART I

MINDSET

1

Why Is Networking Not Taught in Schools?

Learning to network is largely up to each individual business-person because this crucial skill is almost never taught in school—whether that is high school, college, or graduate programs. As speakers and authors, we are troubled by this simply because networking, also what we refer to as referral marketing, is one of the most important ways for entrepreneurs to build their businesses.

A survey we conducted a few years ago with over 12,000 businesses around the world found that 91.4 percent of the respondents said networking played a role in their success. Another survey we conducted with over 1,400 business people revealed that 88 percent of respondents said that they had never had any college course that even covered the topic of networking! To clarify, this question was not about an entire course on the subject (they are almost nonexistent) but any course that simply addressed the topic.

This is unfortunate and a disservice to entrepreneurial-minded students.

Colleges and universities regularly give people bachelor's degrees in marketing, business, and even entrepreneurship, but they teach them hardly anything about the one subject that virtually every entrepreneur says is critically important to their business—networking and social capital (more on social capital later).

Even more bothersome, our experience has been that universities are resistant to adding coursework on networking. Ivan once suggested to the business dean of a large university that the business curriculum should include courses in networking. His response? "My professors would never teach that material here. It's all soft science."

It shocked Ivan to hear it at a progressive major university, even though he had run into this attitude many times at many business schools. We suspect that networking is not taught in business school because most are made up of professors who've never owned a business.

Can you imagine a law course taught by someone who was not an attorney or an accounting course taught by anyone without direct accounting experience? Yet we put business professors in colleges to teach marketing and entrepreneurship with little or no firsthand experience in the field. Is it any wonder, then, that a subject so critically important to business people is so completely missed by business schools?

Moreover, not all business school students realize learning to network can be advantageous, so there is likely little student input on the need for this subject to be taught. Entrepreneurs make up only a portion of business school students; many of the students will work for firms where their ability to get new business is not a key part of their job responsibilities.

Business schools around the world need to wake up and start teaching this curriculum. Schools like any large institution are bureaucracies, so it is unlikely to happen quickly; however, for those schools with vision, foresight, and the ability to act swiftly (sort of the way business professors claim that "businesses" should act); they will be positioning themselves as leaders in education by truly understanding and responding to the needs of today's businesses. These schools will be on the cutting edge of business education so as to better serve their students while positioning themselves as a leading institution for entrepreneurs.

The art and science of networking is finally being codified and structured, which gives us hope that business schools around the world will begin to incorporate it into their curriculum. A thorough bibliography of many of these articles and books can be found in the back of *The World's Best Known Marketing Secret (4th Edition)* by Ivan Misner and Mike Macedonio (En Passant Publishing, 2012).

It is widely accepted among businesspeople that networking is a mechanism that enables their success. As more universities and colleges open their doors to professors who want to include this strategy with their marketing instruction, we are going to see a major shift in the business landscape. We will see emerging entrepreneurs who will be equipped with another strategy for success in business. We will see networking utilized at its fullest capacity, and we will see business schools actually teaching a subject that the business practitioner says is important.

Let's return to the end of Ivan's conversation with the dean and share how it concluded. Ivan asked him, "How are courses on leadership any less a soft science than networking?" He didn't have an answer. The school has since replaced this dean with a new one who believes that emotional intelligence is an important thing to teach our college students. There may be hope yet!

2

Networking Disconnect–Four Ways to Avoid It

Ivan was at a large networking event with more than 900 people recently. When he went up to do his presentation, he began by asking the audience: "How many of you came here today hoping to do a little business—maybe make a sale?"

The overwhelming majority of the people in the audience raised their hands. He then asked, "How many of you are here today hoping to buy something?" No one raised a hand—not one single person! This is the networking disconnect.

THE GREAT DISCONNECT

The networking disconnect is the gap between a person's desire to sell at an event and the attendees' desire to buy.

Think of it like owning a lemonade stand where you feel like you have the best lemonade on the block, and you want to sell it to everyone. All up and down the block there are hundreds and hundreds of other people just like you doing the exact same thing... selling their lemonade.

But here's the thing: no one is looking to buy!

The street is completely empty of potential customers. The only ones there are all the people with all their lemonade stands looking to sell more lemonade.

That's the gap we're talking about.

So if you're going to networking events hoping to sell something, you're dreaming. Networking is not face-to-face cold calling!

Effective networking is about developing relationships. Even if you have occasionally made a sale at a networking event, you must remember that selling at networking events is a rarity. We're not saying it doesn't ever happen. We're just saying it happens about as often as a solar eclipse. Even a blind squirrel can find a nut. Any businessperson can stumble on some business at a networking meeting from time to time. However, when you have most of the people at an event trying to sell and virtually no one there to buy, you're crazy if you think the odds are in your favor to make a sale.

So why go? You go because networking is about long-term success rather than short-term gain. It's about developing relationships with other business professionals. Sometimes you go to a networking event to increase your visibility, sometimes you go to establish further credibility with people you know, and sometimes you may even go to meet a long-time referral partner and do some business and move to profitability. In any case, the true master networkers know that networking events are about moving through a process and not about closing deals.

The question then is this: How do you avoid getting into the "networking disconnect" trap when attending networking events? Here are four strategies you can use to avoid that mistake.

Make It About the Relationship

Networking is not about a transaction; it's about a relationship. It works best when you're striving to make connections that lead to professional contacts. It doesn't work well when you're attending a meeting just to make a sale. The root word of relationship is *relate*. So, relate to them by establishing a genuine connection whenever possible.

Become a Good Interviewer

When you meet people for the first time, learn how to ask questions that get them to talk about their business. Be flexible. Don't just use a script; start with some questions in mind and go with the flow. Ask them about their target market, what they like most about what they do, what's new in their industry, what are some of their challenges in that business, what got them in that profession, and what they like most about the business.

Build a Diverse Network of Referral Partners

Diversity is an important key to building a powerful personal network. Seek out people from diverse backgrounds. You never know who people know. One of the biggest referrals in terms of financial value that Ivan once saw came from a cosmetics consultant who referred a client's husband to a commercial graphic design company. The referral was worth hundreds of thousands of dollars. The irony was that neither the husband nor the graphic design company thought that the cosmetics consultant had the kind of contacts that would put them together. They happily discovered the error of their ways.

Follow-Up

When you meet people at networking events that you want to get to know better, set up a time to have a one-to-one meeting with them later. Remember, the one-to-one should not be used as an opportunity to sell. It should be used to start a business relationship. When you ask for the one-to-one, do so by telling them that you want to learn more about what they do and how you might be able to help them. Of course, you want them to help you—that's important. However, the best way to build a relationship with someone is to find ways to help the other person first. It's counterintuitive, but it works.

People who have had bad experiences with networking are generally victims of the networking disconnect, and it's this disconnect that often gives networking a bad name. It doesn't have to be a negative experience, though. It can be positive if the networking is about the relationship and not about the transaction.

Social Capital

You've heard of financial capital, but do you know about social capital?

Financial capital is the material wealth, whether money or property, that is accumulated by individuals and businesses and used, or available for use, in the production of more wealth. This is the standard definition in economics.

Social capital is the accumulation of resources developed in the course of social interactions, especially through personal and professional networks. These resources include ideas, knowledge, information, opportunities, contacts, and, of course, referrals.

They also include trust, confidence, friendship, good deeds, and goodwill.

Like financial capital, social capital is accumulated by individuals and businesses and used in the production of wealth. Unlike financial capital, social capital is intangible, but it's every bit as real as financial capital. Although it is difficult or impossible to measure precisely, it can be even more powerful than financial capital in terms of eventual return on investment (ROI).

Social capital is built by design, not by chance. According to Wayne Baker, author of *Achieving Success Through Social Capital* (Jossey-Bass, 2000):

> *Studies show that lucky people increase their chances of being in the right place at the right time by building a "spider web structure" of relationships that catch information. Success is social: all the ingredients of success that we customarily think of as individual—talent, intelligence, education, effort, and luck—are intertwined with networks.*

Thus, a key way that social capital is acquired is through the process of networking. Successful networking is all about building and maintaining solid professional relationships. The trouble is that we don't live in *Little House on the Prairie* anymore, and we no longer have these natural community-like business relationships. Many people hardly know their own neighbors, let alone the business people who run the shops and stores down at the local strip mall. Yet, more than ever, networking is critical for an individual's success in business.

BACK TO THE FUTURE

Networking is the kind of social and professional interaction that came naturally to business people throughout most of this nation's history, especially in smaller communities. As villages grew into towns, and towns into cities, and cities into megalopolises, the sense of community, and the close, personal business relationships that went with it, gradually disappeared. The rise of large retail chains and multinational corporations, along with the demise of small businesses under the stiff price competition from these giants, further weakened the natural networking that existed.

The disappearance of community-based networking has left a vacuum that is now being filled by strong-contact networks. Business networking organizations such as BNI create a virtual main street for business professionals—an environment and a system for passing referrals that is the 21st-century equivalent of the traditional model for doing business.

As Eric Lesser, in his book *Knowledge and Social Capital* (Butterworth-Heinemann, 2000), notes, "Without a shared understanding of common terms, activities, and outcomes, it becomes very difficult to reap the benefits associated with building social capital." The power of business networking organizations is that they provide these common terms, activities, and outcomes in a system that is designed specifically to accomplish this goal.

When you join and attend meetings in a business-networking group, you build social capital in a number of ways. You gain the trust and friendship of fellow members; you provide valuable referrals; you contribute knowledge and skills to the effort; you become more knowledgeable and improve your social and business skills. Not least, you get out of your cave—the self-imposed isolation that many business people fall prey to.

Like financial capital, social capital not only is earned and accumulated but can also be spent. This is the idea underlying BNI's guiding principle, Givers Gain®: the good you do comes back to you, over the long term and often in indirect ways. You accumulate social capital by providing help, advice, information, referrals, and other benefits to your fellow networkers with no thought of a quid pro quo. By gaining the trust of others, gratitude for value provided, and a solid reputation for integrity and expertise, you become a person whom others wish to help whenever an opportunity to do so presents itself.

OUTSIDE THE CAVE

Social capital works for everybody, not just people who set out purposefully to become networkers. A colleague of ours works in a profession that entails a minimal amount of day-to-day interaction with others: writing and editing. He handles a limited number of projects, usually no more than two or three books at a time, and works long hours and days in isolation, surfacing occasionally to communicate with an author or publisher about details. You might say he works in a cave with only a few air holes.

How does a cave dweller build social capital? This particular editor, feeling the isolation, crawled out of his cave one day and went looking for company. He joined a small band of writers who were forming a professional organization. Energized, he joined their efforts to build the organization, attract new members, publish a newsletter, schedule presentations and speakers, arrange conferences with editors and agents, and even throw a few parties to lure other writers out of their caves. All of this work was done by volunteers who got a kick out of building a service organization that would help writers network with one another and achieve success.

The organization grew and became the largest networking organization for writers in the nation. While this was happening, our friend the editor made several new friends among the organization's founding members. One of them told him of a job opening that turned into a 12-year-long salaried position; this gave him the steady income he needed to support his family. Another friend, a low-volume publisher of high-quality books, gave him several editing projects and, after his salaried job ended, a full schedule of freelance work.

Many of the authors that this publisher referred to the editor returned again and again with other projects for other publishers.

One of these writers was Ivan Misner, co-author of this book and nearly two-dozen others, on most of which he has worked with the same cave-dwelling editor.

Although the editor didn't know it when he began this low-key form of networking, he was building social capital when he thought he was only having fun. Over the years, the interest on this social capital began flowing back to him in many different forms, with no direct connection to the benefits he had helped provide to other writers.

RELATIONSHIPS ARE CURRENCY

How many times have you seen an entrepreneur (maybe even yourself) go to a networking event, meet a bunch of good people, then leave and never talk to them again? Too often, right? And it's not because he doesn't like them or doesn't ever want to see them again but because he's a busy, busy person with so much going on that he can't even remember what he had for breakfast, let alone reconnect with individuals he just met.

It's a shame because such new contacts are where future business is born.

Don't be misled: it's not the number of contacts you make that's important; it's the ones you turn into lasting relationships. There's quite a difference. Try making ten cold calls and introducing yourself. OK, how well did that go?

Now call five people you already know and tell them you're putting together a marketing plan for the coming year and would appreciate any help that they could provide, in the form of either a referral or new business.

Better results behind door #2, right? Of course. You already have a relationship with these folks, and depending on how deep it is, most of them would be glad to help you.

So here's the question: How can you deepen the relationships with people you already know to the point where they might be willing to help you out in the future? Here are four quick steps to get you moving in the right direction.

1. *Give your clients a personal call.* Find out how things went with the project you were involved in. Ask if there's anything else you can do to help. Important: do not ask for a referral at this point.

2. *Make personal calls to all the people who have helped you or referred business to you.* Ask them how things are going. Try to learn more about their current activities so you can refer business to them.

3. *Put together a hit list of 50 people you'd like to stay in touch with this year.* Include anyone who has given you business in the last 12 months (from Steps 1 and 2) as well as any other prospects you've connected with recently. Send them cards on the next holiday (Memorial Day, Independence Day, Labor Day, etc.).

4. *Two weeks after you sent them cards, call them and see what's going on.* If they're past clients or people you've talked to before, now is the perfect time to ask for a referral. If they're prospects, perhaps you can set up an appointment to have coffee and find out if their plans might include using your services.

See how easy that was? After a few weeks, you'll have more than enough social capital to tap into for the rest of the year. Social capital is the international currency of networking, especially business networking. If you take as much care in raising and investing your social capital as you do your financial capital, you'll find that the benefits that flow from these intangible investments not only will be rewarding in themselves but will also multiply your material returns many times over.

4

The Law of Reciprocity

The term *reciprocity* is at the center of relationship networking, but it is often misunderstood. Webster's dictionary defines reciprocity as "a mutual or cooperative interchange of favors or privileges," as when actions taken for the benefit of others are returned in kind. This leads many inexperienced networkers to expect an immediate return for any actions they take on behalf of another. Givers gain, right?

Wrong. Think of it this way: the first word in Givers Gain® is givers. This is important. It signifies that the act of giving is the first and most important part of the principle. It does not, however, mean that every act of giving will be immediately rewarded by the recipient. On the contrary, the idea driving Givers Gain is, paradoxically, the principle of giving without the expectation of an immediate return.

IT'S THE LAW

In networking, this idea is called the law of reciprocity. The law of reciprocity differs from the standard notion of reciprocity in that the giver cannot, should not, and does not expect an immediate return on her investment in another person's gain. The only thing that she can be sure of is that, given enough effort and time, her generosity will be returned by and through her network of contacts, associates, friends, family, colleagues, and others—many times over and in many different ways.

The law of reciprocity validates the abundance mindset by proving that there is far more business to be gained by referring business to others than you might at first expect. If you go into relationship networking thinking that simply giving a referral is enough to get you a referral in return, you're confusing a relationship with a transaction. As pointed out in *Truth or Delusion? Busting Networking's Biggest Myths*, by Ivan Misner and Mike Macedonio (Greenleaf Book Group, 2006), the law of reciprocity is not simply a quid pro quo; it's providing benefits (including referrals) to others in order to create strong networking relationships that will eventually bring benefits (especially referrals) to you, often in a very roundabout way rather than directly from the person you benefit. This makes the law of reciprocity an enormously powerful tool for growing your own business's size and profitability.

Here are some things to keep in mind as you learn to use the law of reciprocity:

- *Giving means helping others achieve success.* What is your plan to contribute to others? How much time and energy can you spare for this? Do you actively seek out opportunities to help people? You could volunteer to help out with something that's important to someone in your network, offer advice or support in time of need, or even work hard to connect someone to a valuable contact of yours.

● *The person who helps you will not necessarily be the person you helped.* Author, salesman, and motivational speaker Zig Ziglar said, "If you help enough people get what they want, you will get what you want." In other words, what goes around comes around. If you focus intently on helping others, you will achieve success in the end.

● *The law of reciprocity can be measured.* This is our answer to the myth that networking cannot be measured: we use the Networking Scorecard, part of the Certified Networker Program® that's offered by Asentiv. To see how it works, try using the simplified version in Figure 4.1 on page 32 for a few weeks. If you're applying the law of reciprocity consistently, you will see your weekly total score gradually rise. The full version of the scorecard is found on page 265.

● *Success takes getting involved.* Contrary to Woody Allen's assertion that "90 percent of success is just showing up," you have to do more than simply be present to be a successful networker. If you join a chamber of commerce, become an ambassador. If you join a BNI chapter, get involved in the leadership team. If you join a civic organization, get on a committee. The law of reciprocity requires giving to the group; it will pay you back many times over.

THE ABUNDANCE MINDSET

As a businessperson who is just starting to network, you might find yourself in a crisis of confidence in the first few months. You've been attending events, meeting new contacts, collecting business

Figure 4.1
Networking Scorecard Worksheet

Week of:							
Action	**Points**	**Mon**	**Tue**	**Wed**	**Thur**	**Fri**	**Total**
Send a thank-you card	1×						
Send a thank-you gift	5×						
Call a referral source	2×						
Arrange a one-to-one	5×						
Attend a networking event	5×						
Bring someone with you to the networking event	5×						
Set up an activity with multiple referral sources	10×						
Give a referral (level of referral 4× = points)	___×						
Send an article of known interest to someone	5×						
Total							

cards, forming new relationships, handing out referrals right and left, helping other businesspeople solve problems, but receiving no referrals in return. You've been assured that seeing no immediate return isn't unusual, but you are getting discouraged because you've put out all that effort on behalf of other businesses and gained no new clients. You're getting a nagging feeling that it's a sucker's game, that despite your generous efforts nobody else cares what happens to you; you may even feel you've lost ground by neglecting your own business.

So when an experienced networker then tells you to give some business to someone whose business is similar to yours, whose market overlaps your own, your reaction is sheer panic. Give business to a competitor? In what universe?

Businesspeople sometimes feel that there's a strictly limited amount of business to be had and that their job is to corral as much of it as possible at the expense of their competitors. But the fact is that the amount of business, in most cases, far exceeds the available vendor capacity. Scarcity is an illusion.

No two vendors offer exactly the same lineup of products or services to their clients. You and your competitors have different preferences about what kinds of business you provide and what kinds of clients you serve. If you explore the possibilities, you will

IVAN

When I was building my first consulting business, I became involved with a large project that required more than one consultant in my field of business consulting. As a result, I found myself teamed up with a competitor, an arrangement that turned out to be of mutual benefit to us both. My competitor preferred doing budgeting and financial consulting work for our clients, so I handed over that work to him; in return, he sent human resources and strategic planning jobs to me, which pleased me mightily.

After the project was completed, my competitor and I decided we liked the arrangement so much that we kept referring business to each other along the same lines. In fact, we got other professionals involved and formed a power team, a group of businesses that were related to ours but not competing with us and to which it was natural to refer business.

often find that your interests dovetail with those of a competitor, either in your offerings or your geographic service area. By referring your less desirable business to a competitor who prefers it, you can position yourself to receive the competitor's surplus business, the kind you want to get, in return.

Understanding and using this coincidence of interests with your competitors is part of what networkers call an abundance mindset. It is part of the principle of Givers Gain, and it operates according to the law of reciprocity. By giving business to others—in this case, your competitors—you will be rewarded down the line, quite possibly in ways you didn't anticipate or from a source you weren't aware of. There's more than enough business to go around, and this is the principle that underlies the abundance mindset.

A master networker understands that, although networking is not the end but simply the means to growing a business, service to your network of contacts must always be uppermost in your networking activities. Once you have established a solid reputation as someone who cares about the success of others, the law of reciprocity will reward you with an abundance of high-quality referrals.

5

Farming for Referrals

If we could impart one piece of wisdom regarding networking and getting more referrals, it would be this: networking is about farming for new contacts, not hunting them. It's a point that needs to be made, because most business professionals go about networking the way our cave-dwelling ancestors did when hunting for food—aggressively and carrying a big stick.

You'll see them at any gathering of businesspeople. They're so busy looking for the next big sale or trying to meet the "right" prospect that they approach networking simply as an exercise in sifting through crowds of people until they bag the ideal client, the big customer who can turn their business around. They don't have time for regular people like us; they're stalking the director of marketing, chief operating officer, or other high-octane connection, looking for the big kill.

"Farmers" take a different approach. They don't waste time looking for the right person; instead, like those who plant seeds and patiently nurture their crops, they seek to form and build relationships wherever they can find them. If they get an immediate payoff, that's fine, but it's not their principal goal. They know that the effort expended upfront will pay off in a rich harvest later on—much richer than the hunter's quick kill—and that truly profitable relationships can't be rushed.

DROP THE GUN, GRAB THE PLOW

As a business professional seeking to get more business through relationship networking, you need to know the difference between hunting and farming and act accordingly. It's easy to fall into the trap of hunting for the contact who's ready to buy your product or service right now, not six months down the road. We know you're tempted to be a hunter because we're subject to the same pressures. You've got a lot going on, and you need more business right away.

Although we understand the quest for fast money, there's just one problem: it's exactly the wrong approach. Relationship marketing in general and networking in particular is about consistency and reliability: consistently meeting new people and reliably following up with the folks you have just met. It's about developing relationships with referral partners who can provide a steady stream of income far into the future—the opposite of fast money.

This is why thinking of networking as farming is so important. When you're meeting people for the first time, you should be planting the seeds for a lasting relationship. Instead of thinking about whether this person is ready to buy right now, you should focus on developing rapport. Here's how.

Ask the Right Questions

Don't ask qualifying questions, as if you're interviewing a new hire. Questions asked in a veiled attempt to determine whether the person is ready to do business rarely fool anyone; we call them see-through questions because most prospects see right through them.

Instead, ask questions that demonstrate your genuine interest in the other person and her business:

- How long have you been in the business?
- What made you want to start up this business? (assuming she's a business owner)
- What kind of clients do you typically work with?
- Where is your business located?
- What's your geographic coverage?

Offer Free Professional Advice

Let's say you're a real estate agent talking with someone at a networking event who, although not ready to buy a home today, is heading in that direction. You could say something like this:

> Well, I know you're not interested in buying a home right now, but when you're ready to start looking, I'd highly recommend checking out the north part of town. A lot of my clients are seeing their homes appreciate in the 10 to 20 percent range, and from what I understand, the city is thinking about building another middle school in that area.

See how it's possible to offer some value-added advice without being too salesy? A statement like this acknowledges that your prospect is not currently in the market (first sentence) but still demonstrates your expertise so he will remember and perhaps contact you when he's ready to move.

This model works for consultants, CPAs, accountants, financial planners, coaches—just about anyone in a service-based industry in which knowledge is the main product. The concern we sometimes hear from clients is that their knowledge is valuable and they don't want to just give away their intellectual capital.

We agree. You shouldn't have to, but here's the rub: few people will sign up with you if they're not sure you can do the job—and in the absence of a tangible product, you have nothing but your technical expertise to demonstrate that you have the goods. And when you think about it, that makes sense. Whenever you're ready to buy an automobile, it doesn't matter how much research you've done on a particular model, you're probably not going to write your check until you've taken the car for a test-drive.

The same is true for your prospects. Give them a little test drive to show how it would feel to do business with you. If you're a marketing consultant, give them a couple of ideas on how they can increase the exposure of their business. Don't go overboard; maybe offer a technique you read in a magazine or tried with one of your clients. Just give them something they can try on to see if it works.

Not only will this open up a good conversation with the person (while you're out networking), but if you play your cards right, whom do you think they'll go to when they're in need of your kind of service? When it comes to building rapport and creating trust, nothing does it better than solid, helpful information provided out of a genuine concern for the other person.

Provide a Referral or Contact

Try to offer a direct referral (someone you know who's in the market for this person's services) or a solid contact (someone who could help in other ways down the road). Let's say you're networking and you run into a person who owns a printing shop. You talk for a while, you hit it off, and even though you don't know of anyone who's looking for this person's selection of print services right now, you'd like to help him out. So you say:

You know, Jim, I don't know of anyone who's actively in the market for printing services right now, but I do have someone who I think could be a big help to your business. Her name is Jane Smith, and she's a marketing consultant. I know a lot of her clients need business cards, fliers, and things like that printed, and while I don't know if she has a deal on the table right now, I think you both would really hit it off if you got together.

You see how easy that was? You stated right upfront you don't know of anyone in the market right now. You then followed up by saying you do know of someone who you think could help and briefly described how. Chances are, this will sound like a good idea to your new contact.

Be careful; you just met this person and don't want to jump the gun by letting him into your contact database too soon. However, in the rare cases where you feel a connection right off the bat, don't be afraid of pointing him in the direction of someone you know who could help his business.

DOWN ON THE FARM

When you're farming for contacts, it means you're focusing more on the relationship itself than on what you might get as a result of knowing this person. It also means that the way you develop your relationship is far more important than anything your fellow networkers bring to the table.

Once you buy into farming as an approach to relationship networking, you'll find yourself:

- a lot less stressed, since you won't feel the pressure to get more immediate business at whatever networking function you're at today
- more upbeat, since each networking event won't feel like a hit-or-miss approach for getting more business

❽ getting more clients than you can possibly handle, as prospects begin to gravitate to your cool, confident aura without even knowing why

So remember, when it comes to farming for contacts, it's about consistency, reliability, and a genuine desire to get to know the other person. Keep those goals in mind, and in no time, you'll be networking like a pro.

6

How Diverse Is Your Network?

Generally speaking, most networks are "clumpy" (that's the technical term). Human beings, by nature, have a tendency to congregate and surround ourselves with people who are similar to us . . . whether by race, gender, religion, or professional status.

This approach to networking, unfortunately, prompts an unintended consequence. If we aren't intentional about building our network, we end up surrounding ourselves with people who have networks very similar to our own.

Having a network of likeminded people can be a liability for entrepreneurs and business professionals because it seriously compromises our ability to gain access to various companies, organizations, or community groups. It's difficult to network into new organizations when everyone in your network knows the same people!

You know John, Bill, and Sally over at the country club, and so do I. Because we're both members!

I know Jane, Sue, and Steve at XYZ Company, and so do you. Because we both work there!

As a matter of fact, you can make the argument that the more our two networks overlap, the less benefit (defined as new people you and I can interact with as a result of our knowing each other) both of us receive.

HAVE A DIVERSE NETWORK

The scenario above highlights the importance of having a diverse network.

A diverse personal network enables you to increase the possibility of including connectors or "linchpins" in your network. Linchpins are people who in some way cross over between two or more clusters or groups of individuals; this allows them to link groups of people together easily. The best way to increase the number of possible connections in your network is to intentionally develop a diverse, heterogeneous network instead of a homogeneous one.

College alumni networks serve as a perfect example of how valuable linchpins can be. We'll use ourselves as examples. Ivan went to University of Southern California (USC) while Brian went to Duke University. By knowing each other, and being in each other's network, we exponentially increase the number of people we can connect with through our respective networks.

Ivan doesn't have the Duke connection with Brian's alumni friends, and Brian doesn't have the USC connection with Ivan's alumni contacts. By being connected to each other, though, we each are the linchpin to an otherwise out-of-touch group for both of us.

How to Diversify Your Network

Let's look at three ways to diversify your network.

First, find others who are involved with other community groups that you are not.

If you're a member of the Chamber of Commerce and BNI, then a great way to diversify would be to find someone who's a member of the Rotary Club and Parent Teachers Association. This should not be your sole criterion for meeting with someone, but it's a good start by "fishing in a different pond" and meeting people who are not in your natural sphere.

Volunteer more.

This is something we highly encourage not only for the community benefit but also for the diversity it brings to your network. Brian used to volunteer and coach seventh- and eighth-grade boys' basketball. This experience brought him personal fulfillment because he was able to demonstrate a positive male role model by displaying a series of positive characteristics—sportsmanship, accountability, communication, and thoughtfulness—to a group of kids who may or may not have been exposed to that in the past.

And in the process, it also diversified his network. Brian talked to parents and met people who he would never have come into contact with otherwise.

Volunteering in your local community can provide the same benefits to you. Find something that you like doing and see how you can get involved. A quick search online will likely show you several options, and you will be on your way to doing something you love and meeting new people.

Join the board of a local organization. Becoming a board member is not as straightforward as volunteering for an organization because it's not something you can directly seek out. But to the degree that you can, learn what it takes to join the board of a local business community group. Once you've gained this information, take the necessary steps to achieve that goal. For some clubs, like Kiwanis and Rotary, you might get asked to sit on the board after having expressed an interest. Sometimes, letting people know your interest in assuming a leadership role is all it takes.

Gaining a position on a leadership team might also be a good first step if you're unable to become a board member. Regardless, by being on a board or in a different leadership position, you will gain exposure to people you would not normally encounter in your day-to-day networking.

THE BOTTOM LINE

If you want to build a powerful network, realize the value of diversity and branch out. Build a diverse network of professional contacts that include people that don't look like you, sound like you, speak like you, or have your background, education, or history.

The only thing that they should have in common with you and the other people in your network is that they should be really good at what they do. Create a network like that, and it will help you succeed at anything.

7

The Butterfly Effect

You've probably heard of the "butterfly effect"—the theory that a small action in one place can have a ripple effect that creates a dramatic action in another place. The flap of a butterfly's wings is sometimes cited as an example, where the tiny flutter of its wings in one part of the world, through a series of chain reactions, can actually cause a tornado in another. In networking, it is about how a seemingly minor connection or conversation with one person may, after many ripples across the network, end in a high-powered connection later.

IVAN

My first visit to Necker Island in the British Virgin Islands is a vivid demonstration of the butterfly effect. It started several years ago when I received a phone call from Kim George, a woman I didn't know then but who has since become a good friend. Kim asked me if I would be willing to help with the creation of an online networking and social capital community. I agreed to participate because it fit the values and direction I wanted for my company. This was the first flap of the butterfly's wing.

It took time and work to put it together, and our collaboration on this network turned naturally into a strategic alliance, which led to a speaking engagement and allowed me to meet Jack Canfield, co-author of the Chicken Soup for the Soul series. Jack invited me to participate in an international organization: the Transformational Leadership Council. There, I met Nancy Salzman, owner of NXIVM (pronounced Nexium) Training. Nancy got my wife, Beth, and me invited to spend five days on beautiful Necker Island, talking with some of the world's most successful financiers, movie producers, and business leaders, including Sir Richard Branson— world adventurer and founder of the Virgin brand.

Now do you see the tornado taking shape? Wait, there's more.

Sir Richard is the founder of not only Virgin Atlantic Airways but also Virgin Galactic, the world's first private space travel company. Using a two-stage airplane launch system designed by airplane builder Burt Rutan in Southern California, he plans to ferry private astronauts, science packages, and payloads into suborbital space within the next few years. At the end of our visit on Necker Island, Richard invited us to attend the rollout of this new aerospace system in Mojave, California.

A few months later, we were flown from Los Angeles International, via a Virgin America charter plane named My Other Ride Is a Spaceship, to the Mojave Spaceport. There in the windswept desert at the base of the Sierra Nevada Mountains, we witnessed the unveiling of WhiteKnightTwo, the astounding twin-fuselage "mothership" that will carry SpaceShipTwo aloft and launch it into space. It was an otherworldly experience.

At the party in Bel Air later that evening, Burt told me that he expects the cost of space tourism to drop to a fraction of its current cost once all the systems are in place. He also expects Virgin Galactic to open a space hotel; that set me thinking about holding business networking meetings in orbit. I told him I thought that was a bold long-term vision. He said, "That's just our midterm vision. Later, we'll have private space trips from the earth to the moon and back."

And the tornado goes on spinning. Who knows where it will stop?

Thus, a simple telephone call from a fellow networker led me over the course of a few years to a networker's dream—the chance to hobnob with world movers and shakers on a Caribbean island and to see the launching of the private space travel industry. It demonstrates vividly how a seemingly insignificant contact can lead you to connections and relationships that may well surprise you when you look back to where the journey started. When the butterfly flaps its wings, you never know where you'll end up, but if you're on your toes, you can ride the whirlwind to success.

There is one other salient fact about Ivan's butterfly that he did not mention: it raised his value as a networker by at least a few notches. Who wouldn't want to have a networking partner who can connect with Sir Richard Branson, Burt Rutan, and all their connections? You never know whom they know. (Caution: before you ask Ivan for these contacts, make sure you are at the high end of C (credibility) with him. See Chapter 9: Your Network Should Be Both Wide and Deep for more on that.)

8

Do Referrals Happen by Accident?

A few years ago, a long-standing member of a business networking organization was talking about canceling his membership—not because he wasn't getting enough referrals but because he was getting too much business.

That's right. Despite a full year of getting great referrals, Steve's friend Mike didn't feel that the results proved that networking was a viable business strategy for getting more referrals. He felt that the business he had gotten was based on "chance occurrences"—one person knowing another, who happened to know him—and despite the fact that he kept getting these referrals as a result of his networking contacts, it couldn't possibly last. So he left the group.

Even though Mike's misguided reasoning led him down the wrong road, it raises a good question, and understanding the answer could help your business. The question is simply this: despite the chance nature of networking, is meeting more people something you can count on as a consistent means of getting more business?

Mike's challenge boiled down to two things: repeatability and understanding. His training told him that the way to get more business was to target a certain kind of customer by calling people from a demographics-based list. If he didn't have enough business, he needed to make more calls. How many more? He could figure that out, too, because the amount of business he got was directly proportional to the number of people he talked to. It was a repeatable process that he fully understood.

On the other hand, clients he got from referrals always had a story line that he couldn't see being repeated. Sally knew Jim, who ran into Sue, who happened to be in his group and referred Mike the business. This led Mike to conclude that the results were coincidental and couldn't possibly be repeated.

Mike's reasoning wasn't entirely off track, as far as it went. If you focused on the specific people who gave you the referral, rather than the process and relationships that allowed it to happen, then no, you couldn't consistently get more business from networking. Or, to put it another way, Sally knowing Jim, who ran into Sue, who ultimately gave Mike a referral is probably never going to happen again in exactly that way. But if you step back and ask, "Is it possible that somebody will know someone else who's looking for my services and will then give me that referral?" Well, that's a whole other story—especially if you focus on building relationships so that there's always a somebody.

What led Mike astray was this: he was thinking about hunting when he should have been thinking about farming.

IVAN

When it comes to networking and passing referrals, it's not about who's giving what to whom. At no point in this book do we say, "For every referral you give, you can expect one in return." Nor do we say that when you hand out more referrals, other business professionals will automatically do the same. It just doesn't work that way.

Think of referral giving in the context of the abundance mindset (see Chapter 4: The Law of Reciprocity), which is the awareness that there's more than enough business to go around. If you hear of a business opportunity that would be well suited for a referral partner—in other words, not your kind of business, but hers—think of it as excess business. When you pass this kind of excess business to others in the form of a referral, you'll wind up attracting more prospects who want to work with you.

Call it an act from the referral gods, but when you do good things for others, those good things have a habit of making their way back to you—often from a different person or group of people. Even if it seems that you're not benefiting from the referrals you're giving to others, take note of all the other business that "just happens" to come your way:

- the guy who stumbles across your website and gives you a call
- the old prospect you haven't heard from in months who suddenly wants to get together for lunch
- the inactive client who wants to renew his contract with you

> Even though it seems like happenstance, some or all of that is likely to be new business you attracted by giving away other business (in the form of referrals) to people you know.

The process of meeting people, staying in touch, and then asking for their business is something you can do time after time. You don't have to worry about how a specific referral got to you because you understand the process of growing your network and developing your relationships.

And here's the best part: your network can be working for you all the time. You don't have to be there whenever someone you know runs into someone else who could use your services because the whole process works without you. This is especially true when you've become a referral gatekeeper and have begun to get referrals not only from your own network of contacts but also from the networks of others.

When it comes to networking, there is no coincidence about referrals. They're the inevitable cumulative result of the day-to-day activities of relationship building. And even though they can't be measured as easily as cold calls, the results are far more powerful.

Now that you have the right mindset for networking, the remainder of this book provides you with actionable tools to build a rock-solid foundation for profitable business relationships. By the end, you'll have a clear understanding of the entire process that produces referrals, rather than an undue concern over the exact chain of events leading to a specific piece of business. Once you understand that, be warned: you will have more business than you can handle.

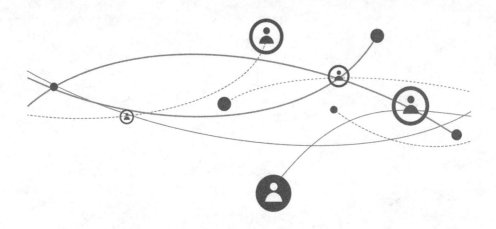

PART II

YOUR NETWORKING STRATEGY

9

Your Network Should Be Both Wide and Deep

People sometimes make the mistake of building a network or group of contacts that's "a mile wide and an inch deep." In other words, they like the idea of knowing as many people as possible, which in and of itself isn't a problem. However, the depth of those relationships—how well they know each person— is shallow.

Getting to know someone at a deeper level might not sound like a legitimate goal because doing so might feel more like an effort to make new friends instead of getting new business. But people are often surprised at the positive results of having both a wide and deep network. Seemingly meaningless details have the power to solidify a growing relationship.

MAKE CONTACTS THAT COUNT

When you're considering asking someone in your personal network for a favor, ask yourself if she's a contact or a connection. A contact is someone you know, but with whom you haven't fully established a strong relationship; a connection is someone who knows you and trusts you because you've taken the time to establish credibility with her. Among the most important connections you can make are those with your referral sources, with prospects these referral sources bring you, and with customers you recruit from the prospects.

You may have a lot of contacts, but how well do you know them, and how well do they know you? It's unrealistic to expect help from contacts who don't know you well and feel no loyalty to you. If you're spending a lot of time going out and meeting new contacts, think about how much more profitably your time might be spent if you devoted more of it to turning existing contacts into connections.

The more people you know, the broader your network; the better you know them. You can't know everybody equally well, of course. Just as some of your friends are closer to you than others, you will have deeper relationships with some of your networking partners than with others. These are the people you know best, people you believe and trust, people to whom you don't hesitate to offer help and referrals whenever you see the opportunity, and people you trust and count on to promote your business to their clients, to cross-market your products or services, and to give you high-quality referrals.

MAKE IT PERSONAL

Forging a deep connection with a potential referral partner starts with a genuine desire to get to know the other person. And we're talking about the whole person, not just the superficial information

IVAN

I think the absolute master at creating a deep network is Harvey Mackay, a speaker and bestselling motivational author. The first time I spoke to Harvey on the phone, he must have been taking notes about everything I said. The second time I had a conversation with him, Harvey surprised me by asking, "So, how are your kids? You've got three, right? What are Ashley and Cassie doing now? And how's Trey doing—is he about ready to go to college?"

I was thinking, "Wow! How did you remember all that?" The more I spoke to Harvey, the more I became convinced that he had a system for keeping track of the important details of the people in his network.

Now when I talk to him, I know what he's doing, and I love it! I'm especially impressed by Harvey's system because it takes work. He has a database of the people in his network, and he does some research before calling anyone. He's continually adding and updating the information—your pets' names, your children's names, your birthday, and the anniversary of your company startup. Harvey sets himself apart by putting in an effort to honor people by remembering what's important to them. It's hard not to be impressed by that.

you might hear during their elevator pitch. We're talking about things like:

- Details about their family (number of kids, names, etc.)

- Interests and how they like to spend their spare time
- Business goals/aspirations (things they really want to accomplish)

You must be careful when having a conversation that elicits this type of information because you don't want to come across as giving people the third degree, and you want to respect the fact that this is a business environment. For Brian, he "greases the wheels" by sharing information about himself first.

When talking to someone at an event, Brian might share that he enjoys watching sports (basketball and football, specifically), has a dog, plays golf, and spends a ton of time watching movies on Netflix. (And depending on how long the conversation goes, he might even offer a recommendation or two!)

The point is to show people his willingness to share and talk about himself in a way that goes beyond just the regular back and forth you might have at networking events.

The result is a good start at a potentially deep relationship with the person.

Contrary to what many people initially think when hearing this advice (people are sometimes skeptical), starting a relationship this way helps people grow their business through word of mouth.

THE GAINS PROFILE

BNI uses a tool called the GAINS profile—it stands for "Goals, Accomplishments, Interests, Networks, and Skills." Before rolling it out, we tested its effectiveness on a small group of people. Each person filled out the profile, listing their goals, accomplishments, interests, networks, and skills—both personal and professional. Two men in our test group balked at the idea, proclaiming it was "silly." We reminded them that they were part of a test group for a reason—we wanted to know whether the tool worked or not.

Appeasing us, the two skeptics shared their goals, accomplishments, interests, networks, and skills with each other. During the process, they discovered that they were both coaches for their sons' soccer teams. All of a sudden, these men were best friends! They talked about soccer, sharing plays with each other. They even ended up scouting out the competition for one another's teams.

And guess what happened? Within three months of the GAINS exercise, they were passing quality referrals to each other. Prior to participating in the test group, the men had never done business with each other even though they had known each other for a year. The change happened because they found out they were both soccer coaches and that game connected them. That connection built trust, which turned into business.

Connecting over a nonbusiness interest endears you to the other person. Now, you're not just some salesperson—you're a friend.

Ivan knows a businesswoman named Laura who has always wanted to travel to Greece. One of her networking connections learned of Laura's dream trip, which prompted her to buy Laura two simple items as a "thank you" for something she did: a calendar of beautiful places in Greece and a coffee-table book about Greece. They soon became fast friends! The business associate's thoughtfulness caused the relationship to deepen because she gave Laura tangible proof of her recognition and support of her goal. You pay a compliment to people when you show that you understand what's important to them. Make it an aim of yours to learn at least one goal or personal interest someone has outside of their business.

10

Building Quality Relationships Through the VCP Process

As most people know, quality business relationships don't just happen overnight. It starts with meeting that person for the first time, then maybe meeting them again under different circumstances (e.g., coffee connection or at another networking event).

After that, depending on how strong a connection was made, it has the potential to blossom into a full-blown business relationship where you would consider yourself friends.

It's during this time where you really trust this person, and hopefully vice versa, and referrals are coming and going between the two of you.

This, in a perfect world, is the goal of your networking activities: to reach a level of "probability" between the two of you.

But as we said before, this is a process that develops over time and involves three distinct phases: visibility, credibility, and profitability. We call this the VCP Process®.

VISIBILITY TO CREDIBILITY TO PROFITABILITY

The VCP Process describes the creation, growth, and strengthening of business, professional, and personal relationships; it is useful for assessing the status of a relationship and where it fits in the process of getting referrals. It can be used to nurture the growth of an effective and rewarding relationship with a prospective friend, client, co-worker, vendor, colleague, or family member. When fully realized, such a relationship is mutually rewarding and thus self-perpetuating.

Visibility

In the first phase of growing a relationship, you and another individual become aware of each other—that is, visible to each other. In business terms, a potential source of referrals or a potential customer becomes aware of the nature of your business, perhaps because of your PR and advertising efforts or perhaps through someone you both know. This person may observe you in the act of conducting business or relating with the people around you. The two of you begin to communicate and establish links—perhaps a question or two over the phone about product availability. You may become personally acquainted and work on a first-name basis, but you know little about each other. A combination of many such relationships forms a casual-contact network, a sort of de facto association based on one or more shared interests.

The visibility phase is important because it creates recognition and awareness. The greater your visibility, the more widely known you will be, the more information you will obtain about others, the more opportunities you will be exposed to, and the greater your chances will be of being accepted by other individuals or groups as someone to whom they can or should refer business. Visibility must be actively maintained and developed; without it, you cannot move on to the next level, credibility.

Credibility

Once you and your new acquaintance begin to form expectations of each other and the expectations are fulfilled, your relationship can enter the credibility stage. If each person is confident of gaining satisfaction from the relationship, then it will continue to strengthen.

Credibility is the quality of being reliable, worthy of confidence. Credibility grows when appointments are kept, promises are acted upon, facts are verified, and services are rendered. The old saying that results speak louder than words is true. Failure to live up to expectations—to keep both explicit and implicit promises—can kill a budding relationship before it breaks the surface of the ground and can create visibility of a kind you don't want.

To determine how credible you are, people often turn to third parties. They ask someone they know who has known you longer or perhaps has done business with you. Will that person vouch for you? Are you honest? Are your products and services effective? Are you someone who can be counted on in a crunch?

Profitability

The mature relationship, whether business or personal, can be defined in terms of its profitability. Is it mutually rewarding? Do both partners gain satisfaction from it? Does it maintain itself by providing benefits to both? If it doesn't profit both partners to keep it going, it probably will not endure.

BE PATIENT

The time it takes to pass through the phases of a developing relationship is highly variable. It's not always easy to determine when profitability has been achieved: A week? A month? A year? In a time of urgent need, you and a client may proceed from visibility to credibility overnight. The same is true of profitability; it may happen quickly, or it may take years, but most likely it will be somewhere in between. It will depend on the frequency and quality of the contacts and especially on the desire of both parties to move the relationship forward.

Shortsightedness can impede the full development of the relationship. Perhaps you're a customer who has done business with a certain vendor off and on for several months, but to save pennies you keep hunting around for the lowest price, ignoring the value this vendor provides in terms of service, hours, goodwill, and reliability. Are you really profiting from the relationship, or are you stunting its growth? Perhaps if you gave this vendor all your business, you could work out terms that would benefit both of you. Profitability is not found by bargain hunting. It must be cultivated, and like farming, it takes patience.

Visibility and credibility are important in the relationship-building stages of the referral marketing process. But when you have established an effective referral generation system, you will have entered the profitability stage of your relationships with many people—the people who send you referrals and the customers you recruit as a result. It's an essential part of successful relationship marketing and networking.

11

Where Networkers Gather

Business professionals who don't have a lot of spare time on their hands often ask us which networking groups provide the biggest bang for their buck. We tell them that there are five main types and that what works best depends on the business they're in and the prospects they want to meet. Here's a quick rundown of the most familiar types.

FIVE TYPES OF BUSINESS NETWORKING ORGANIZATIONS
1. Casual Contact Networks
Casual contact networks are general business groups that allow many people from various overlapping professions. There are no

restrictions on the number of people represented in any profession. These groups usually meet monthly and often hold mixers where everyone mingles informally. Casual contact networks may hold other meetings to listen to guest speakers present on important business topics or to discuss issues concerning legislation, community affairs, or local business programs.

The best examples of these groups are the thousands of chambers of commerce that are active across North America and elsewhere in the world. They offer participants an opportunity to make valuable contacts with many other business people in the community. By attending chamber mixers, presentations, and other activities, you can make initial contacts that will be valuable in other aspects of developing your referral business.

But because casual-contact organizations are not tailored primarily to help you get referrals, you have to exert effort to make them work. For example, you can volunteer to be a chamber ambassador, a position that that requires little time commitment but provides much exposure. Sitting on committees helps you get to know members better, especially the ones who devote the most time to the organization and are therefore good candidates to become diligent, conscientious members of your own network. Most of all, you need to attend regularly so you can take advantage of every opportunity to strengthen the relationships you do form. You can find your local chamber by calling information in your area or by contacting the U.S. Chamber of Commerce at www.uschamber.com.

Some people have told us that they did not get much business by "networking" in their local chamber. When asked whether they attended mixers regularly, sat on any committees, attended the networking breakfasts, met with the executive director, or volunteered to be a chamber ambassador, they always said, "No." Well, guess what—networking is a contact sport!

If you want to build your business through referrals, you must be willing to get out of your "cave" and make ongoing, effective contact with other business people. Just being a member is not enough. You must make meaningful contact with the other participants, as regularly as possible.

Participating in chambers or other networking groups means working your way to higher levels of responsibility within the organization. This includes taking on leadership roles, serving on the board, or being an ambassador. Remember the VCP Process®. These roles give you an opportunity to make more contacts and move these contacts into solid relationships faster.

2. Strong Contact Networks (e.g., Referral Groups like BNI)

Organizations whose purpose is principally to help members exchange business referrals are known as strong contact referral groups. Some of these groups, BNI for example, meet weekly, typically over lunch or breakfast.

Most of them limit membership to one member per profession or specialty. If you're a CPA and join a local BNI chapter, then you'll have locked out the competition by joining; no one else can fill the CPA category in that chapter. Each weekly meeting usually lasts about 90 minutes, and you might want to stay another half-hour or so to network afterward and solidify your relationships with other members of the group.

A typical meeting usually includes:

- Open networking
- Short presentations by everyone
- A longer, more detailed presentation by one or two members
- Time devoted solely to passing business referrals

Strong contact networks provide highly focused opportunities for you and your associates to begin developing your referral marketing campaigns. You won't meet hundreds of business people in this type of group, but all the members will be carrying your business cards around with them everywhere they go. The net result is like having up to 50 salespeople working for you! With a program like this, you will be establishing powerful long-term relationships that will prove invaluable.

If you are considering a strong-contact group, then you'll want to keep in mind a couple of things.

- You need to have a schedule that lets you attend all or almost all of the meetings. Regular attendance is vital to developing a rapport with the other members of the group and getting to know their businesses. Otherwise, how can you generate a referral for someone if you don't know him or what he does? How is anyone going to get to know you better and generate referrals for your business? Attending every weekly meeting must be a priority. The good news is that since most of these meetings are held in the early morning or at lunch, they won't intrude too much on your day.

- You have to buy into the team approach that defines these organizations. You need to feel comfortable going to a networking event and being on the lookout for prospects who can help other members of your group. This can be counterintuitive for some, since businesspeople are usually focused on their own business. For example, if you're a real estate agent and you find out that someone just moved into a new home and is no longer in need of your services, you need the presence of mind to ask about other areas in this person's life where someone else in your group could help (e.g., electrician, handyman, lawn service). This can be a little tricky at first, but the group will be watching what you do—take our word for it. A good strong-contact networking group typically tracks the amount of business that is conducted. BNI, for example, tallies the total number of referrals from the previous week, the amount of revenue attached to that total, and a couple of other metrics that give visitors and members alike a sense of how the chapter is progressing. If you're not "pulling your weight" in the group, you'll be asked to leave or referrals will stop coming your way.

However, when you do add value to the group by inviting visitors, passing referrals, and being a conscientious business professional (all things that are outlined in New Member Training), then you'll be well on your way toward building a rock solid, referral-based business.

3. Community Service Clubs

Another type of networking group is the service club. Unlike the more business-oriented groups discussed previously, the service

A Look at BNI (Business Network International)

BNI was created in 1985 as a way for business people to generate referrals in a structured, professional environment. The organization has grown to thousands of chapters worldwide and has generated millions of referrals for its members.

The primary purpose of BNI is to pass qualified business referrals to the members. This is accomplished by developing strong business relationships within each chapter. Each chapter follows a structured agenda that includes presentations from the members and distribution of qualified business referrals at each meeting. These referrals are tracked and recorded by the chapter officers in order to gauge the activity and success of the chapter. For more information, go to www.bni.com.

A Look at Rotary International

Rotary, the world's first service club, can be described in many ways. Functionally, Rotary is an association of local clubs gathered into a larger organization called "Rotary International." The individual member is a member of his local club; all clubs are members of Rotary International.

Officially, Rotary is defined as, "An organization of business and professional men and women united worldwide, who provide humanitarian service, encourage high ethical standards in all vocations, and help build good-will and peace in the world."

Specifically, a Rotary Club is composed of business and professional men and women in a community who have accepted the ideal of service as a basis for attaining fulfillment in their personal, vocational, and community lives. Tens of thousands of Rotary Clubs meet weekly, usually for breakfast, lunch, or dinner.

Originally, Rotary was, "To promote the 'scientizing' of acquaintances as . . . an aid for success," but this early credo was dropped long ago. Although Rotary Clubs, as well as the other major service clubs, are now focused primarily on providing public service to their local communities, business is definitely conducted with fellow members. Today, there are thousands of Rotary Clubs throughout most of the world. For more information, go to www.Rotary.org.

(*Source*: Focus on Rotary, by Rotary International)

group is not set up primarily for referral networking; its activities are focused on service to the community. However, as a practitioner of the Givers Gain philosophy, the master networker is a natural fit. In the course of giving time and effort to civic causes, you form lasting relationships that broaden and deepen your personal and business networks. If you go in not to benefit but to contribute, the social capital you accrue will eventually reward you in other ways and from other directions—business among them.

With any business organization, but particularly with service clubs, it is crucial to remember that making effective contacts is a journey, not a destination. In other words, it is not something you do for a while and then stop—it is a process that you must continually follow.

IVAN

In 1986, I had been a member of a service club for only two months. At one luncheon meeting, the club president announced that a community center project in town was short on funds and that the fund-raising committee was seeking donations to finish construction. It seemed like a highly worthwhile project, so I got out my checkbook and began to write a check for $50. As I was writing, the president introduced two members of the club, both seated at my table, who had just donated $50,000 each! I closed my checkbook and slipped it back into my coat pocket very quietly. I didn't want anyone at the table to see that I had been writing a $50 check, when two of them had just donated a combined total of $100,000. At that very moment, I decided that these were very nice people to be having lunch with on a weekly basis.

Years later, when I had developed strong relationships with various members in this service club, I was lamenting to some of the members at my lunch table how I couldn't get a good mortgage rate on a particular property I wanted to acquire. One fellow at the table said to me, "Well, how much are you looking for?"

"$150,000," I said.

"I've got $150,000," he replied. "When do you need it?"

"Are you kidding me?"

"No, I'm serious. I've known you a long time, and I have some money that I can invest. When do you need it?"

"Next week would be OK," I said.

"OK, fine. We can draw up an agreement next week."

"Will there be any points?"

"No, no points," he said. "Not among friends. Tomorrow we can work out the details."

The following week, we wrote up an agreement, and I had the money, just like that. Well, I really shouldn't say, "just like that," because I had laid the groundwork with several years of participation in this service club. As one of his committee chairmen, I had helped this individual when he was club president, and we got to know one another during this time. If that hadn't happened, there would have been no chance of him trusting me enough to loan the money.

4. Professional Associations

Professional associations have existed for many years. Association members tend to be from one specific type of industry, such as banking, architecture, personnel, accounting, or health. The primary purpose of a professional association is to exchange information and ideas.

Your goal in tapping into such networks is to join groups that contain your potential clients or target markets. A simple procedure for targeting key groups is to ask your best clients or customers which groups they belong to. This will give you an immediate list of at least three to five, and probably as many as 10 to 12, groups from which to choose.

Your best customers retain membership in the associations that offer the greatest value or for which there is some key strategic or competitive advantage. Similarly, the prospects you wish to target may, in many ways, operate like your best customers and have many of the same needs.

Joining such a group is like being a kid in a candy store: all that business is potentially within reach. Many groups, however, limit their membership to those who have specific industry credentials, and vendors aren't welcome (that is, if you want to join an association of accountants, you have to be an accountant).

To generate more income or to give their full members a well-rounded slate of potential vendors, a growing number of professional associations have created an associate member category. Associate members are not active in the business or profession for whom the group was formed.

In associations that allow vendors as members, you're likely to encounter considerable competition. Many people have the same idea that you do. Sometimes, full members are turned off because so many vendors have approached them.

Instead, we recommend you stand out by finding ways to help them without selling to them. As an example, if you were a social media consultant and you joined an association of professional business coaches, rather than trying to "sell" them on your services, how about volunteering to run the association's social platforms? You don't have to go crazy, but taking charge of their Facebook (www.facebook.com) and LinkedIn (www.linkedin.com) pages would be a great start toward building relationships and showing them your value.

Obviously, every business is different, but take a minute to figure out how your business might be able to help others in a particular industry association and then go do it!

Conversely, if you join a group that represents your profession (and not your target market), you can still make contacts that might lead to shared opportunities with people in your profession who have a slightly different specialty or need assistance on a large project. You never know where a good referral might come from, so don't ignore this as a possible opportunity.

At the very least, a professional association of peers enables you to evaluate the marketing materials and presentations of others. By taking a good look at what works for others, you may be able to improve your own brochures, cards, or presentations.

Here are examples of professional associations:

- American Society of Personnel Administrators
- Certified Life Underwriters Association
- National Association of Professional Organizers
- American Bar Association
- American Medical Association
- National Speakers Association

A simple Google search on professional associations in your field or target market should give you a good starting point for researching the one's that appeal to you.

5. Online/Social Media Networks

From a business perspective, the ideal use for social media is to build your brand and your credibility with the people you are connected to; it's about providing value for your connections and followers. It is important to offer them useful information balanced with a little personal insight, and—whether you're talking about face-to-face networking or online networking—credibility and relationship building is still critical to the process.

With social media, the key to success is outlining a strategy that considers the amount of time you can realistically dedicate each day to your online marketing efforts and being consistent. People have a tendency to be online at random times, start clicking away, and then something mysterious happens to the "space-time continuum" and all of a sudden two hours go by, and they have nothing to show for it! Here's how to avoid falling victim to that trap: have a plan and work it! Write up a plan for how often you will work your social media and for how long.

Sit down and map out a weekly schedule that outlines specific days and times that you will spend developing your social media strategy. Figure out what's realistic and what makes sense for your company and go from there.

For example, if you use Facebook, LinkedIn, and Twitter for your social media marketing, then put it down on a schedule. Maybe Facebook posts go out Tuesday and Thursday afternoons, while LinkedIn happens Wednesday and Friday mornings. And Twitter might be something you use for just when you see good stuff out there on social media and you want to quickly distribute it.

The point is to leverage your time! Be sure to utilize the various tools currently available that are designed specifically to save you time in your social media efforts. For example, sites like SmarterQueue (https://smarterqueue.com), Hootsuite (https://hootsuite.com), and Buffer (https://buffer.com) are designed to send your social media updates to multiple social networking sites, including Twitter and Facebook, with one click.

Some sites even allow you to link multiple Facebook and Twitter accounts (if you have more than one) to one desktop application where you can post updates to all sites, as well as view and respond to your friends' posts on those sites and keep a log of all your past posts. This means no more logging in to multiple social networking sites—you can manage all your social networking accounts from one place!

Once you have your strategy in place, you will no doubt be anxious to start seeing a return on your social media investment. It's vital to remember something we mentioned before: networking is more about farming than it is about hunting, whether online or face to face. It's about cultivating relationships with people. The bottom line is—it takes time. It is about building the credibility of your brand and that doesn't happen overnight.

ROI is directly correlated to 1) dollars spent (online paid marketing) and 2) time and/or effort spent in saturating and building strong profiles on whatever social media channels are deemed effective for the brand (including blogging). Don't forget that some businesses will benefit much more from spending more effort on "niche" networks that may have less traffic but are more targeted to the brand's ultimate consumer.

If your network is a mile wide and an inch deep, it will not be successful. It is important that you create a network that is both wide and deep. You do this by being visible and engaging in the conversation. Over time, this will give you credibility, which leads to building your brand and your sales, and will ultimately provide you the biggest ROI for your online marketing efforts.

CHOOSING THE NETWORKS THAT ARE THE BEST FOR YOU

Despite all we've covered thus far, some people tell us they simply don't have time to go to business meetings regularly. We understand that objection well. If you feel this way, let us suggest that you throw away this book, pick up your telephone, and start making cold calls instead. Or, if you prefer, open your checkbook and start writing checks for more advertising. If you're serious about developing business by referral, there is no quick fix: you must meet people in a planned and structured way.

Which groups should you join? Don't let chance decide where you're going to spend your time and effort. Remember, the key is to diversify your activity. Don't put all your eggs in one basket; one type of business organization won't serve all of your needs. Consciously select a well-rounded mix of organizations, with no two of the same type. If you have associates, partners, or employees, consider their participation when deciding which groups each of you will target.

12

Online Networking: Click Here to Connect

We talked about the importance of online networking via the internet in previous chapters, but let's take a deeper look at what it might mean for you—and for traditional business networking itself.

For the record, we believe in online networks. We also believe online networking is not a panacea and that anyone who wants to network like a pro should include it as one of her core strategies—but not rely on it solely. Online networking has strengths and weaknesses. You have to be aware of both its upside and its downside to use it most effectively.

From the most veteran networkers to the newest newbies, questions about web-based opportunities and platforms abound. Could online networking replace face-to-face contacts? Does online networking differ from face-to-face networking in certain key aspects, besides the obvious fact that contact is made through a computer? Who is best suited to online networking? The list goes on.

LOOKING PAST THE HYPE

Before we address those questions and more, allow us a few observations. The wow factor of constantly changing social networking techniques and technologies has grabbed people around the world in ways we couldn't have imagined years ago. From politicians and celebrities, to grandmothers and grandchildren, sites like Facebook, Twitter, LinkedIn, and others have transformed the way many people reach out and communicate.

Online communication is here to stay, but it won't stay still. It's dynamic. It's evolving. And it's democratic, with a small "d," in that online networking literally flattens the communication hierarchy. It enables you to bypass many different organizational levels and filters to communicate with—or jump over—all levels, from top to bottom, making a CEO directly accessible to a temp toiling away in the supply room.

It's pretty exciting stuff. After all, most of us love new toys no matter what our age! They're fun. They're novel. They sometimes help us attract new friends into our circle, especially if the toy can be shared.

Now, we're not about to claim that online networking platforms are toys—far from it. But, you have to admit, there are some beguiling parallels: fun . . . novel . . . attract new friends. The line between playful interaction and business-building camaraderie can get blurry—all the more so on the web, where it's often easy to waste more time at a faster rate than in the offline world.

Our point: Avoid getting carried away by all the e-buzz. Hype is kind of like the fluffy meringue on a pie: yummy and fun but no substitute for a nutritious meal.

Because humans tend to be social creatures and love new toys, we're not surprised that technology today lets us socialize and play in new ways. Understandable enthusiasm for the latest MyBiz FaceSpace site, however, will turn out to be nothing more than an e-distraction unless you have clear purposes in mind for its use.

MIND THE FUNDAMENTALS

How do we stay on track, keeping our business acumen sharp, while nodding knowingly at the sirens of social networking? The best compass for online navigating is the simple, old-fashioned notion "Know thyself." Go back to basics: what do you want from networking? What are you willing to put into your network relationships?

The fundamentals of networking apply—in spades—online. The three stages of the VCP Process—visibility, credibility, and profitability—are as relevant in the online world as they are in face-to-face networking. If you try to bypass the first two stages and get to profitability first, you produce something nobody likes or respects: spam!

There's a confidence curve you have to negotiate before trying to do business with someone. If you take that curve too fast, you'll flip your reputation and end up in a very awkward position. This is especially hazardous in the online realm, because a few words on a computer screen can be interpreted entirely differently than in a face-to-face setting.

IS FACE-TO-FACE COMMUNICATION OUTMODED?

One of the questions we encounter regularly from networkers and would-be networkers is this: now that we have [fill in the blank with the online social networking space of your choice], doesn't that spell the end of traditional, face-to-face networking? Our answer: No!

As we've said before, online communication is a great tool to integrate into your networking, but online doesn't replace face-to-face contact. There are aspects of networking that are simply better face to face: you can see an expression, hear a tone of voice, and shake a hand. The nuances of communication and personality conveyed through face-to-face interaction just don't translate well online.

Videoconferencing has made great strides in the past few years, and it has opened the doors for many small businesses truly to be international. Applications like Skype (www.skype.com), which provides call clarity and screen-sharing abilities, can help you conduct business. Other tools like GoToWebinar (www.gotomeeting. com/webinar) and Zoom (https://zoom.us/) facilitate fully remote conferences that allow for hundreds of participants. These tools are tremendous for building strong relationships with remote colleagues and clients, but never pass up the opportunity to meet someone in person. Especially for local businesspeople, a virtual meeting is no substitute for a good networking event.

Business networking is about relationships—hopefully, relationships that lead to reciprocal gain—and because relationships depend on both verbal and nonverbal language, face-to-face contact is irreplaceable. Business-building relationships require depth, trust, and a real understanding of participants' needs, wants, and expectations.

CONNECTING WITH PEOPLE AT WEB SPEED

The best online social media experts understand clearly that face-to-face contact in business is irreplaceable.

To be candid, we love social media. We are both active on social media. We have found that social media is fantastic for "brand building"—and we also know that social media will not replace all marketing efforts for most entrepreneurs and salespeople. In fact,

IVAN

While I was in Stockholm giving a presentation on networking, a Swedish newspaper reporter arranged to do an interview with me. I agreed, and when he arrived for the interview, he really started putting me on the spot about online networking, telling me it was replacing face-to-face contact. He was pretty militant about his point of view and was essentially telling me that traditional networking was going the way of the buggy whip.

Well, I was a little annoyed and surprised that this reporter was being kind of confrontational about networking. So I finally asked him: "Why are you here to do this interview?"

He seemed confused and asked, "What do you mean?"

I said, "Why did you drive all the way out here to this big stadium to meet with me in person just for this interview?"

He looked at me and said, "Interviews are better face to face."

And I said, "Exactly! I rest my case."

"Networking is much the same," I told him. "It beats communicating online, or over the phone, because nothing can ever fully replace an in-person conversation."

The reporter relented. "Yeah, I get it," he said. "That makes sense. Some things are much better in person."

That's right: some things are better in person, and networking is one of them. This doesn't mean that online networking isn't valuable—far from it. Online networking is a powerful tool in our arsenal of networking strategies. However, it shouldn't be the only tool we use because sometimes it's simply not the best one. For me, the bottom line regarding face-to-face networking vs. online networking is that I don't think it should be an "either-or" scenario; I think it should be a "both-and" scenario if you want to build a strong personal network.

Until the time comes when we can have a face-to-face meeting with a holographic image like the Jedi Knights of Star Wars, it's probably still a good idea to network in person whenever possible. By the way, when the world does advance to a point where we can do the *Star Wars Networking* thing, I want to be Obi-Wan Kenobi. I'm just saying.

for most businesses, it just does not generate a large percentage of their new business.

We know, we know, there are people out there right now that are officially apoplectic. Take a deep breath. Know that we love you and we love social media. It has been a fantastic tool for us to retain our audience and keep them engaged. It has been great as a brand builder. We've also seen the data, and it is sobering.

Here's a great example. In 2011, the Freelance Industry Report did a thorough survey of the industry. One of the many questions they asked was "What has been your most effective method for finding and landing clients . . .?" Four of the top five answers all related to networking (word of mouth, referrals, personal/professional network, local networking). These added up to 69.5 percent of all business development for the respondents. Social media ranked as eighth with 2.8 percent. But wait, that's not the most amazing thing. When asked about where they would spend more time and resources in the upcoming 12 months, social media ranked first with 46.1 percent!

But wait, that's still not the most amazing thing about this story. You see, when the 2012 report came out, the networking-related choices for how respondents actually generated their business that year, now moved up to 74.3 percent! But where was social media you ask? Well with all their commitment to focus more time and resources on social media, the report found that the respondents had moved the needle to 2.8 percent . . . oh wait, it was 2.8 percent in the previous year! So here's the most amazing part of the story: despite their commitment to put more time and resources on social media to generate their new business the following year, the respondents actually did not move the needle at all. Zero. Zip. Nada.

And now the really crazy thing—in 2012, 42.8 percent of the respondents said that next year they were going to focus more on— you got it—social media again! There's a saying for this: what's the definition of insanity? Doing something over and over again and expecting a different result.

In two separate reports, these business professionals were generating 70 percent or more of their business from networking. They generated less than 3 percent from social media. Don't you think that it would be a good idea to increase their networking efforts as well? We do. That's one of the reasons we feel a book like this is so important.

Even if online technologies don't generate much new business, they do facilitate quick and convenient communication. Ivan and his staff at BNI use a service that enables them to distribute one message simultaneously to Facebook, Twitter, LinkedIn, and a panoply of other social networking sites. He and his staff send four or five quotes a week via a platform that spares them from having to log onto all of those sites separately—a huge time saver.

Similarly, Ivan and his team use RSS feeds (RSS is short for real simple syndication) from his blog to push updates out to his pages on Facebook, LinkedIn, and others. That way, people who have connected to or followed him can get the feed quickly and automatically.

IVAN

Social media lets us directly communicate with those who are interested in hearing what you say, and technology flattens the communication hierarchy.

When I started my company 30 years ago, it cost an exorbitant amount to talk to people in other states, and it even cost money to call across town. Just to put that in perspective, in 1986, my telephone bill was the second largest business expense. (Salaries were number one.)

Today, I can make calls across the country for literally pennies and do conference calls with those in other countries, online for free.

Social media platforms are a big part of that, since I can now talk directly to my audience and bypass all of the "middlemen."

These technologies let you communicate directly with people who are interested in hearing what you have to say. My friends—the members of my audience—are all over the world, so I can say something that I want to communicate globally and get the message out in the blink of an eye.

WHERE SOCIAL AND FACE-TO-FACE NETWORKING MEET

Even though this book is more about face-to-face networking than it is online, we still wanted to delve into the ever-growing area of social media and online networking. And since we ourselves are not the experts in that area, we brought in someone who is: Mari Smith. She is a premier Facebook marketing and social media expert thought leader. Below is an interview we conducted with her.

How do you see social media integrating with face-to-face networking?

I love that social media allows us to discover new, wonderful people to reach out to connect to. We can build what I call "virtual rapport," and then when we meet our online friends and contacts for the first time, it's like we've already met. In addition, prior to attending an in-person event, I love to do research on fellow speakers and attendees by looking at the event website and hashtag on Twitter. At times, my team and I will create a Google spreadsheet so that I have a short list of key contacts I want to meet at certain events. I'll add notes in real time to the spreadsheet to help my team, and I follow up efficiently afterward.

Do you think it's fair to say that one of the main benefits of social media is brand building?

Absolutely! Everything we do online and on our social sites in particular can either add or detract from our brand. It's vital that we're conscious and kind about our choice of words and images. I'm always strategic. I give a great deal of consideration to each and everything I publish online. Businesses of all sizes need to take control of their own brand management. But, for small- to medium-sized businesses in particular, we need to be ever mindful of how our actions and content may be perceived by others.

A lot of people say that social media is really good for acquiring direct business; I'd be interested in hearing your take on that.

The right activity on Facebook, primarily, but also on Twitter, Instagram, and LinkedIn, can yield tremendous lead generation and sales. The key to success on social media is to think and act like a member first, and then a marketer second. That is, consider the mode your audience is in when they are surfing their Facebook newsfeed: they're in social mode. They see updates from their close friends, family members, high school buddies, and some colleagues and extended communities. Topics are typically fairly personal, from someone announcing news of their new baby to getting engaged, going on vacation, or sharing a personal tribute to a lost loved one. So, as a business person, when crafting our content for organic or paid reach, it needs to have a personal, authentic feel. Storytelling is one of the most powerful ways to do this—share your own story, how your business started, spotlight customers, vendors, go behind the scenes, etc. Content also needs to be what Facebook calls "thumb stopping." As users scroll fast on a mobile, your content needs to speak to them with compelling visuals and relevant messages. Videos and live broadcasts perform particularly well on Facebook. Tie all this to strategy calls-to-action along with a budget for amplified reach and you're bound to see business growth results. (It may take some additional knowledge, though, and I'm a big advocate of seeking professional support and training!)

With so many different online media platforms available, where do you suggest business professionals focus their social media efforts?

I encourage business professionals to really focus on one social network and go deep on it. For most everyone around the world, this has to be Facebook. It's the biggest platform by far with almost 2 billion users now and has the most granular ad targeting features available anywhere online, bar none. Certainly, you want to have an optimized profile on other networks—for B2B, then for sure LinkedIn. (Although, Facebook is rapidly catching up to be the go-to platform for B2B as well as job-hunting and recruiting). And, even if you don't publish much content, at least have your username and bio filled out on Twitter and Instagram—possibly even Pinterest if you're more on the retail side and your audience is primarily women.

What do you think has changed the most in social media today compared to say five years ago?

The number-one thing that's changed for business professionals, in particular, is it was much, much easier to build a large audience faster on Facebook and Twitter five years ago. Plus, in 2012, Facebook had only just gone public and were still fairly generous with their organic reach. Since then, it's plummeted to an all-time low of 1 to 6 percent on average. That is, for every one of your coveted fans (likes) on your Facebook business page, only 1 to 6 people are seeing your content organically. It's pay-to-play. We have to embrace this and not push back. The good news is that it's never been easier to reach the exact, laser-targeted audience with Facebook and Instagram's vast array of targeting tools and ad products.

With pictures and videos becoming an increasingly large chunk of social media today, where do you see social media heading over the next five years?

It's going all video streaming and all mobile. That is exactly what Facebook has stated. It's hard to believe they would be "all mobile," and I doubt they'll ever not have their desktop version. However, keep in mind that over 90 percent of Facebook users access the platform predominantly on mobile devices. So, what is coming is digital streaming television. And Facebook is encouraging more and more celebrities and businesses to build for mobile and to embrace live video. Facebook is definitely the next-generation cable TV. In late summer 2017, Facebook plans to begin releasing a dozen television-quality, original shows that they have bankrolled.

Facebook is essentially entering the market to compete with likes of Netflix (even though Netflix co-founder and CEO Reed Hastings sits on the board of directors at Facebook), Amazon Prime TV, YouTube Red, and Hulu. I also understand Spotify has plans to release a video subscription service. What all this means is these giant companies are rapidly moving into the television advertising industry, which generates over $73 billion in the U.S. alone and more than $175 billion worldwide. Facebook has big designs on that revenue! The company has already begun testing mid-roll ads of 5 to 15 seconds in both video-on-demand (recorded, uploaded videos on the site) and live-streaming video. The big difference between watching shows on television only vs. watching via Facebook, is users can easily choose to watch episodic content on their mobile devices and/or use Facebook's app to stream on their large-screen television.

We are at an exciting new chapter with Facebook—it's like getting in to YouTube ten years ago. Business professionals have a fairly short window of opportunity right now to build up their own television-quality live broadcast and establish thought leadership with sizable followings.

DETERMINING YOUR ONLINE NETWORKING STRATEGCY

Who is best suited for online networking? On the one hand, the answer is obvious: anyone with a computer and an internet connection can access the growing number of social networking sites on the web.

The less obvious answer, however, is based on you and your interactive and time management preferences. Do you enjoy spending time on your computer? Some personality types avoid computer-based interactions as much as possible, while others seem drawn to their monitors, tablets, and phones like moths to light bulbs. There's no right or wrong about it, just degrees of preference. The more you like browsing the internet, communicating via email, and otherwise working digitally, the more likely you are to find online networking a good fit.

If online living isn't your thing, don't despair. Remember, web-based networking is a means to an end. A little time online can be leveraged to great effect when you use that time for connecting briefly with new contacts you'd like to meet in person or for following up after face-to-face encounters.

Consider in advance how much of your time—as in how many hours per day or week—you are truly willing to devote to online networking, as well as how you prefer to use that time (i.e., reviewing discussions in online forums, keeping your profiles updated, posting to your blog, reading and responding to comments, reading other people's blogs, tweeting, and so on).

Which online networking platform is best for you? Many are available, so pick the one(s) where your target audience hangs out most. At the time of this writing, Facebook, LinkedIn, and Twitter are the places to go.

Who knows what another five years will bring? But regardless, go where your folks are!

No matter how many sites you're active on, be very clear with yourself—and with others—about your motives and goals. Stay positive, informative, and value oriented.

Learn the difference between interactions that move you and your online community members toward productive relationship building and those that simply suck time and energy. For example, if someone asks a question that you can answer, that's an opportunity to be helpful while displaying your knowledge. Be careful, though, when comments veer into opinion because you can easily make an offhand remark that goes viral—and that you will regret within seconds. There's no pulling something back once it's in cyberspace, and the audience for your unintended remark can grow exponentially.

Above all, as with any kind of business networking, your objective is to develop social capital. Here's a question you'll have to confront in the online world: will your investment of time, energy, and caring on behalf of other networkers be reciprocated in ways that you find meaningful? Only you can define what meaningful means to you, and only you can decide whether your investment is productive.

OTHER WAYS TO COMMUNICATE ONLINE

As we've said before, blogging and publishing an online newsletter can complement your online networking. Both can also be time-consuming, as the material must be updated regularly to remain current—both in content and in the minds of your audience. So, proceed carefully and deliberately if you choose to launch either or both of these communication tools.

A blog offers your audience a place to get to know you better, but it works as intended only if your target audience itself spends the time to read it. The best blogs are written with their readers (as opposed to their authors) in mind and fill a specific need. For example, blogging about your thoughts on foreign policy works only if you happen to be involved somehow in foreign affairs and can write authoritatively for an interested audience. Blogging about what you had for lunch today will probably interest people only if you are a restaurant critic or at least writing for an audience of ardent foodies.

Books and websites on blogging abound, so educate yourself before diving in. But use caution: a blog is so easy to start today that you could fall into the "ready, fire, aim" trap and get sidetracked into

NETWORKING LIKE A PRO

an activity that ends up being a tangent rather than a core strategy of your online networking.

Much of what we said about blogging applies equally to online newsletters: know your audience and what it wants. Write for your readers and not for yourself. Know why you're publishing it, too. Are you hoping to sell your products or services, build your brand, keep people coming back to your website, alert readers to the latest developments in your company, or fill an information gap? Online newsletters can help you engage with your target audience and generate support and interest—when they're well conceived and well executed.

Decide on your newsletter's frequency in advance. If you're not sure about certain elements of it, start with it monthly so you can learn as you go without inflating expectations. Increasing the frequency to satisfy audience demand is much better than having to decrease frequency because of low interest or other problems.

Publishing an enewsletter requires decent writing skills, the willingness and ability to learn the ropes (i.e., software, design and formatting, collecting and managing email addresses), and a long-term commitment to getting out a quality issue on time, every time.

A CORE STRATEGY THAT'S WORTH KNOWING

Make no mistake about it: the VCP Process still applies to online and social media networking.

In other words, if the relationship is not kept in mind, people will begin to view your overtures as spam.

But if done right, with the proper respect and consistency, social media can be a legitimate tool in branding and raising the awareness people have of you in the business community.

CHAPTER 12 / ONLINE NETWORKING: CLICK HERE TO CONNECT 93

CHAPTER

13

Developing Your Target Market

One of the biggest mistakes we see business professionals make is trying to be everything to everyone. In other words, they have a great product and terrific service and in their minds everyone should be a client.

Yet this approach can make marketing in general, and networking in particular, problematic because businesspeople then don't know where to focus their efforts. They lack strategy.

As an example, if you're a health coach, then everyone really could be your client. You have a great nutritional program and access to a convenient, state-of-the-art gym. Who wouldn't want to lose a few pounds or gain a few pounds of muscle, with a fun, energetic coach? If you have that mindset, everyone could be a client.

But where do you start networking? Everywhere?

Of course not. You don't have the time, money, or energy to do that. So where do you focus your networking efforts? Start by "staying in your lane" by getting a clear idea about who your ideal clients actually are. We call that "spheres of influence" or target markets.

Even if your initial response is to cringe at the thought of limiting your target market, stick with us. We hear your concern, but here's the thing: When you try to be everything to everyone, you wind up being very little to anyone.

Additionally, if you recognize that some clients are easier to get then others, then trying to be everything to everyone actually makes your job harder rather than easier.

Returning to the health coach example, who do you think would be an easier client to get: someone who is 20 pounds overweight and was recently diagnosed with a heart condition or someone who is around 5 pounds over their ideal weight but doesn't think it's a big deal? Again, both people could be clients, but one is much more likely to work with you than the other.

The culprit behind this everything-to-everyone approach is a scarcity mentality. This is the idea that you don't want to miss a sale, any sale, because you never know when the next one is going to make itself available. In other words, you are focusing on not having enough or there not being enough. In our context, the fear of not enough pertains to a fear of not enough clients.

SPHERES OF INFLUENCE

But when you're networking like a pro, you don't have to worry about missing sales, or not getting enough clients, because you're coming from a place of abundance. You're deepening relationships with a variety of people across diverse networks. While referrals still don't just happen by magic—you do have to put consistent effort into those relationships—the business you get from them is much more consistent.

We attribute this consistency to spheres of influence that allow you to better focus your resources in the areas that are most likely to provide success. A sphere of influence is a group of people who are most likely to work with you. Notice the language: "people who are most likely to work with you."

There is no room for everyone in a sphere of influence. A sphere of influence will lack everyone but will be abundant in people who are currently facing a problem that your service has the potential to solve.

Here are steps to determine your spheres of influence.

1. Take a look at your past and current clients, and see who you enjoyed working with the best.
2. From that list, see what they had in common. Was it a type of business/industry you worked with, a type of problem you helped solve, or maybe a specific type of person/personality type you engaged? Look for similarities.
3. Write down two or three spheres of influence based on those results.

So as an example, your spheres of influence might be:

- Women entrepreneurs
- Medical service professionals (doctors, dentists, and chiropractors)
- Corporate executives
- A specific industry or business
- Service professionals (CPAs, lawyers, etc.)
- Millennials
- Salespeople
- Women executives

As you can see, the list is practically endless, and you can pick two or three based on your own experience!

BRIAN

I was doing a presentation in North Carolina a few years back for a group of recruiters and staffing companies. Times were tough. The economy wasn't doing so well and businesses simply weren't hiring a lot of staffing or recruiting companies.

When I walked into the room, there were about 30 people present, all but one of them coming from recruiting and staffing agencies. You know who the other person was? An insurance agent who targeted staffing and recruiting companies as a niche market. Apparently, he'd made the business decision some time back to target that particular group, and he'd been networking with them ever since.

Whom do you think 80 percent of those recruiters and staffing company folks used for their insurance needs? You got it—that one insurance agent. I'm sure staffing and recruiting companies weren't his only target market (it's better to have two to three), but even if they were, there had to be several other chapters within driving distance of his business. Couple that with the state, regional, and annual conferences all trade associations have, and you can see that this insurance agent could have had his hands full while networking only with people who were in his target market.

And once you establish two or three target markets that leverage the inherent strengths of your company and focus your networking there, what you'll find is that your prospects will start calling you with their business. Why? Because you obviously know your stuff and are willing to spend some time to get to know them.

Building your business is all about leveraging your strengths within the context of your prospects' needs, and then networking with as many of those people as you can. It might mean talking with some of your friends and family ("Hey, I'm rolling out a new program that has me talking to a lot of business equipment companies. Would you happen to know of a person who works for a business equipment firm here in town?"). It might also mean attending every industry-specific association meeting within a 50-mile radius of your office. Or it could be both. But what it doesn't mean is running all over town, networking with anyone who happens to be in the room—that's sure to be an exhausting way to acquire new business.

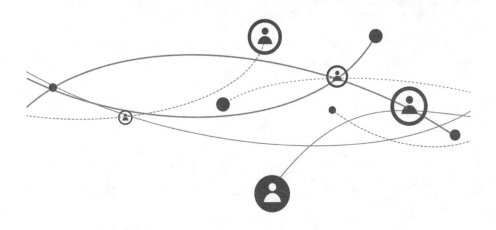

PART III

NETWORKING FACE TO FACE

14

Seven Characteristics of a Great Networker

Many people offer advice about what it takes to be good at networking (ourselves included). This advice, however, often lacks a key piece of information: what the average person thinks it takes to be a better networker. Networking involves interacting with others, so what do most businesspeople think it takes to successfully network? Let us underscore the importance: we all need to be cognizant of other people's expectations and adjust our behavior accordingly if we want to make a positive impression that will help build a powerful network.

THE SEVEN CHARACTERISTICS THAT MAKE A GREAT NETWORKER

We gathered almost 3,400 survey responses from businesspeople around the world who represent both genders (57 percent men, 43 percent women) and ages that span a person's entire career. Six percent of respondents were under 30 while 2 percent were over 70. The bulk of respondents (78 percent) were between the ages of 30 and 59. We gave them a list of roughly 20 different characteristics on networking and asked them to pick the top behaviors they would like to see in a great networker. From those responses, we identified the top seven characteristics of what people believe makes a great networker (see Figure 14.1 on page 105). Here are those seven characteristics in order of importance according to the survey respondents.

1. *Good listener*. Being a good listener tops the list. Our success in networking depends on how well we can listen and learn. The faster you and your networking partner learn what you need to know about each other, the faster you'll establish a valuable relationship.

   A good networker has two ears and one mouth and should use them each proportionately. Listen to people's needs and concerns, and find opportunities to help them. You can't help others if you don't know what they need, and you find out what they need by listening. In many ways, networking is about connecting the dots, but to do that, you have to listen so that you can help people make the connections they are looking for.

2. *Positive attitude*. The first thing that people see from you is your attitude, how you handle yourself day in and day out. A consistently negative attitude makes people dislike you and drives away referrals; a positive attitude makes people want to associate with you. Positive business professionals are like

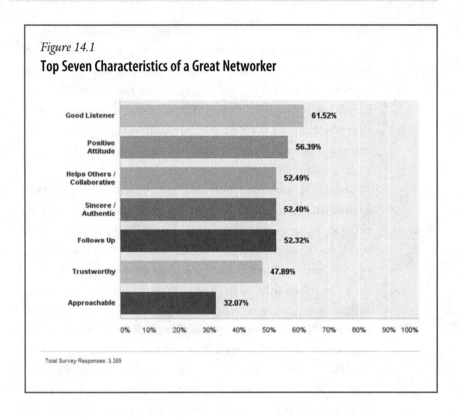

Figure 14.1

Top Seven Characteristics of a Great Networker

Good Listener — 61.52%
Positive Attitude — 56.39%
Helps Others / Collaborative — 52.49%
Sincere / Authentic — 52.40%
Follows Up — 52.32%
Trustworthy — 47.89%
Approachable — 32.07%

0% 10% 20% 30% 40% 50% 60% 70% 80% 90% 100%

Total Survey Responses: 3,389

magnets—others want to be around them and will send their friends and family to them.

3. *Helps others/collaborative.* People don't care how much you know until they know how much you care. Helping people shows that you care. One survey respondent said, "people want to network with individuals who have a collaborative attitude." Helping others can be done in a variety of ways, from emailing a helpful article to someone to putting them in touch with a person who can help with a specific challenge.

Several respondents commented about not wanting to network with people who are "in it for themselves." A willingness to collaborate and help others is essential as it builds trust and helps establish a strong relationship.

4. *Sincere/authentic.* You can offer the help, the thanks, and the listening ear, but if you are not sincerely interested in the other person, they will know it! Those who have developed successful networking skills convey their sincerity at every turn. One respondent stated, "it's all about the authenticity" that someone shows you. We have all seen people who are seemingly good at networking but lack sincerity. Faking it isn't sustainable—and it doesn't work.

5. *Follows up.* If you offer opportunities, whether a simple piece of information, a special contact, or a qualified business referral, to someone who consistently fails to follow up, you'll soon stop wasting your time with this person. One respondent said that when it comes to networking, "the fortune lies in the follow-up" and that many people just "don't follow up anymore."

6. *Trustworthy.* One respondent said it best: "it doesn't matter how successful the person is; if I don't trust them, I don't work with them." When you refer someone, you are putting your reputation on the line. You have to be able to trust your referral partner and be trusted in return. Neither you nor anyone else will refer a contact to someone who can't be trusted to handle it well.

7. *Approachable.* One respondent said that people "will forget what you said and what you did, but they will never forget how you made them feel." In other words, when you are approachable, people feel comfortable. When they feel comfortable, relationships are born. That's why effective networking always starts with approachability.

Each one of the characteristics above tie into the notion of farming not hunting. It's about building mutually beneficial business relationships. Only then will you succeed in creating a powerful network.

15

The Five Least Important Skills to Be a Great Networker

Just like knowing the characteristics of a great networker, it's also important to know what not to do when networking. In this chapter, we walk you through the five least important skills needed to be a great networker, according to the responses from our survey of 3,400 business professionals. We are happy to report that introverts have reason to breathe a sigh of relief when taking in these results.

Most people assume that being an extrovert is an advantage in networking, but let's take a good look at the bottom five characteristics. Four out of the five least important skills to be a great networker involved being outspoken or bold (characteristics more aligned with an extrovert than an introvert). See Figure 15.1 on page 109.

WHAT MATTERS LEAST

Based on the survey, the fifth least important skill for networking was being "fearless." Extroverts tend to be more fearless and confident, but when people identified the skills of a great networker this was not very important.

The fourth least important skill was "asking for the sale." Extroverts almost always ask for the sale more quickly than an introvert. Yet, most people think this skill is not essential to being a great networker.

The third least important skill was being a "self-promoter." This particular result initially seems counterintuitive. How can self-promotion not be an important skill for great networkers? Well, the answer is easy: for networking to be effective, it has to be about the relationship, not the transaction. Many, many people get this one wrong. We think it is the single biggest reason why some people hate networking. They go to a networking event and have one person after another try to sell to them. Very few introverts can be called self-promoters, so this is one more example where being an introvert is not a liability to networking success

The second least important skill was "directness." This survey result is thought provoking because being direct in your business dealings is often considered to be an attribute. However, when it comes to networking, it seems to be viewed more as pushy, which is clearly not a strength in building relationships. Again, extroverts are more inclined to come across as direct than introverts.

The least important characteristic of a great networker, based on this survey, was in many ways very surprising. It was an attribute that could easily apply to both introverts and extroverts: "social media savvy." We included this in the survey because we have found that many people think that networking online is almost all they need

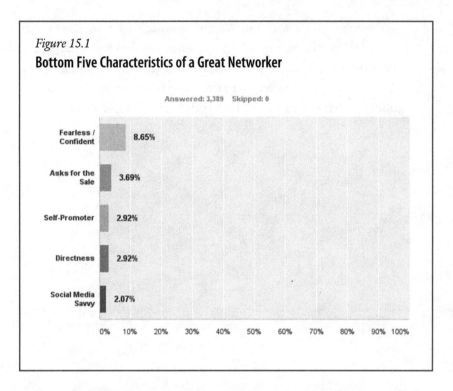

Figure 15.1
Bottom Five Characteristics of a Great Networker

Answered: 3,389   Skipped: 0

Fearless / Confident	8.65%
Asks for the Sale	3.69%
Self-Promoter	2.92%
Directness	2.92%
Social Media Savvy	2.07%

0%   10%   20%   30%   40%   50%   60%   70%   80%   90%   100%

to network effectively. We believe that online networking has great value, but it does not replace face-to-face networking. However, even we were surprised that it ranked dead last by 3,400 businesspeople all around the world.

After viewing this data, we thought surely, a younger generation would rank this characteristic much higher. So, we compared the survey responses of people under 30 to this result. We discovered that there was in fact, a difference. The "under 30 crowd" ranked this characteristic second to last!!! Seriously, second to the last. Even young businesspeople, who are prone to be tech savvy, understand that social media skills are not an indicator of great networking ability.

Understanding what most people consider to be the seven best and five least important characteristics of great networkers can help you improve your networking strategy—and even boost your confidence if you are an introvert. Our evidence clearly shows that introverts are not at a disadvantage when networking. If anything, our results made us stop and pause to consider the implications for extroverts. This combination of knowing what to do as well as knowing what not to do will help you to network like a pro.

16

Top Five Most Common Networking Mistakes

Oftentimes, people who diligently work toward becoming strong networkers still have shortcomings and face disappointments. Even though they understand concepts like the relationship economy and Givers Gain—and even try to implement them—they sometimes don't get the results they expect, and then wonder, "Does networking only work for certain people in certain businesses?"

Absolutely not.

We believe the relationship economy and the Giver's Gain model are universal principles that transcend businesses and cultures. Networking is an equally effective tool no matter what the business or country you're in. It's universal in nature.

Yet, networking seems to work better for some people than it does for others. Why?

In our experience, the culprit usually lies in one of the following five areas. If your networking is not working as well as you'd like, a quick tune-up in these areas should get you back on track. And to clarify, whereas we previously addressed the five least important skills to HAVE for networking, these are the mistakes people commonly MAKE.

LACK OF FOLLOW-UP

Not following up after networking tops our list of worst networking mistakes. Most people have made this error because they get caught up with their other work responsibilities. It's an innocent blunder, but not following up is not only a mistake but also counterproductive. You'd be better off NOT networking in the first place than you are networking and not following up with the people you meet. (Yes, it's that bad.)

Remedying this mistake is all about putting a system in place so you form a habit after each networking event you attend. Brian equates this to packing your gym bag the night before—doing so sets him up to make it to the gym the next morning. Later in the book, we give you concrete steps to implement a process and start forming this habit that will help you bring your business to the next level.

UNCLEAR UNIQUE SELLING PROPOSITION

Ineffectively presenting your business and its value—the unique selling proposition (USP)—is detrimental because people need to understand what you do in order to successfully pass business your way. You can attend the all networking events you can find, but if no one understands what you do or the services you offer, then you are wasting your time—and it's one of the most common mistakes business professionals make.

We recommend your USP follows a simple formula:

"I work with [target market] to help them [benefit]."

Brian's unique selling proposition is succinct and direct: "I help busy entrepreneurs market their business in less than 90 days." That formula leads people to ask not just Brian but also anyone else using the formula, "Well, how do you do that?"

The unfolding of the conversation naturally leads Brian to discuss his business and what makes a good referral for him. It works for him, and it can work for you too.

Remember, if you can't easily and succinctly state your USP, you have a problem. We talk about USPs in much more detail in Chapter 23: Telling Your Company's Story, but for now, just know that a properly constructed USP can go a long way to curing your networking blues.

CONFUSING NETWORKING WITH FACE-TO-FACE COLD CALLING

For this mistake, we need to start with a discussion of the difference between networking and cold calling. Networking is all about relationships and, more specifically, developing them to the point where a reciprocal referral relationship exists. Cold calling is something different. Cold calling is about volume and, more specifically, is about making as many calls as you can, in the hope that "something sticks."

And while neither of us subscribes to the cold-call approach, we're not saying that it can't work or is "bad" in the absolute sense. It's just different.

People get into trouble when they insert a cold call approach in a networking environment. At an event, they immediately try to "work the room" in an effort to meet as many people as possible in hopes that "something will stick."

Hence the term, face-to-face cold calling.

If you find yourself talking to many people at a networking event, handing out cards to everyone, then you might want to reevaluate your overall approach to networking. Remember, networking is about relationships and getting to know people. It's about asking good questions and finding out how you might be able to help each other out. And most of all, it's about developing a rock-solid foundation where future business can be generated. THAT's how you network like a pro.

And while other approaches are perfectly fine in their own right, just remember that if you want to successfully drive referrals in today's relationship economy, you need to have the right approach going in.

NOT RESPONDING QUICKLY TO REFERRAL PARTNERS

This mistake is particularly troubling because we find the very idea of not immediately responding to a call from a networking partner bewildering. Unfortunately, it seems to happen with some regularity. Not long ago, someone we know had a referral for a woman in his networking group. He called the networking associate and left a voicemail as soon as he knew the referral was viable. A day went by without a return call, so he called again saying it was important to connect.

He was finally able to speak to his networking associate at their next meeting. When he asked the associate why she did not return his call, the associate said, "If I knew you had a referral for me, I would've called you back immediately." Our contact did give the referral at the meeting and, to no one's surprise, the referral ended up working with another vendor because no one got back to him in a timely manner.

Treating each of your networking partners as one of your "best clients" is critical. You should always return phone calls from these people immediately, as it speaks to your credibility and reliability as a professional.

There have been countless examples of people receiving referrals at networking groups who go back to their places of business and finally get around to contacting the referral in a few days. The old phrase "if you snooze, you lose" is apropos here. Time is of the essence, and if the referral knows that you had her name and number on Monday and you took your sweet time calling, that sends a message you don't want to be sending!

ABUSING THE RELATIONSHIP

There are many ways that we've seen networking partners abuse the relationship, but the following story is one of the most glaring examples of this situation.

A woman we know was invited to attend a 50th birthday party of an associate who used to belong to a networking group in which she also participated. They once had a long-term working relationship, and so out of respect, she decided to attend.

When she got to the door, she looked through the window and noticed that people were arranged in a semi-circle listening to a presenter in front of an easel board. When she stepped in, it was obvious that the "party goers" were being recruited for a business opportunity. As resentful as the woman felt, she and other mutual friends found it difficult to remove themselves from the "birthday party" despite the fact that the only refreshments being served was the company's diet shake!

Never, ever mislead your networking partners (for that matter—never mislead anyone). Trust is everything in relationship networking. Inviting these people to a "birthday party" that turns out to be a "business opportunity" is not being honest with the people with whom you want to build a trusting relationship.

THE BOTTOM LINE

Take heart that most people have made these networking mistakes before; networking is not something you learn in school or see modeled from most companies around the globe. Networking is what separates successful business professionals from their less successful counterparts. If networking has not been working for you, see what adjustments or changes you can make in your style and approach based on these five mistakes—and suggested course corrections.

Our collective experience lets us happily share that once you iron them out, the world of referrals and mutually beneficial relationships will beat a path to your door.

17

Four Behavioral Styles to Know When Networking

ave you ever met someone at a networking event and immediately hit it off? To the point where even though you're meeting and talking for the first time, it feels like you've known each other forever?

Or maybe you've had the opposite happen. Have you ever run into someone while networking and after three minutes you're thinking to yourself that this isn't "your type of person"?

Well, part of that has to do with the behavior styles of yourself and the people with whom you are networking.

Allow us to explain.

When it comes to behavioral styles, according to *Room Full of Referrals* by Tony Alessandra, Ivan Misner, and Dawn Lyons, there are four basic constructs that we find useful to talk about: Go-Getters, Promoters, Nurturers, and Examiners.

And while most people have elements from all four, there is a tendency for one or two to be a person's most dominant behavior type. This is why, depending on your behavioral type and that of the other person, you can either "hit it off" right away . . . or not.

But here's the thing: as someone who's looking to build their business through word of mouth, relationships are king. This means that regardless of your "natural" personality, it's important to at least understand how to best interact with ALL kinds of people—those similar and different to you—because you never know how any one individual will impact the growth of your business.

So with that in mind, let's take a closer look at each behavioral type, along with some ideas on how you can best interact with people from each one.

GO-GETTER

Definition: A hustling, enterprising type of person.

Go-Getters tend to be very results-oriented, driven, fast-paced, and impatient. They have a "get it done now" attitude. They attend networking events to gain new business and look to meet the most successful people at the event.

Go-Getters believe in expedience and are not afraid to bend the rules. They figure it is easier to beg forgiveness than to ask permission. They are so focused that they can appear aloof. They are so driven that they forget to take the time to smell the roses.

When working with Go-Getters, make sure to:

- Cover "high points" quickly . . . don't follow a script
- Keep conversations interesting by alternating questions and offering relevant information

- Show how they can save time, generate results, and make life more efficient
- Present two to three options with a short summary
- Deliver on everything you promise

PROMOTER

Definition: An active supporter, someone who urges the adoption of or attempts to sell or popularize someone or something.

Promoters tend to be very positive, friendly, and "happy go lucky." They love to be on the go and are okay with having lots of irons in the fire. They avoid confrontations and seek fun in everything they do! They attend networking events to hang out, meet new people, talk to their friends, and make sure they are "seen" at the event.

Promoters would rather "schmooze" with clients over lunch than work on a proposal in the office. They are idea people and dreamers who excel at getting others excited about their vision. They are risk-takers who are not inclined to do their homework or check out information and base many of their decisions on intuition.

When working with Promoters, make sure to:

- Move quickly with an upbeat, playful approach
- Strike a balance between listening to their stories and gathering information you need
- Show how your solution would increase their prestige, image, or recognition
- Agree on specifics in writing
- Reinforce their decision by giving plenty of assistance immediately after the sale

NURTURER

Definition: Someone who gives tender care and protection to a person or thing, especially to help it grow or develop.

Nurturers tend to be very patient, kind, caring, and helpful people. They are great listeners and tend to enjoy things at a slower pace than the Go-Getters and Promoters. They do not like to be pushed or rushed into things, and they appreciate quality time with people. They attend networking functions to connect with people they already know, meet a few down-to-earth people, and focus on deepening their relationships.

Nurturers' relaxed dispositions make them approachable and warm. They develop strong networks of people who are willing to be mutually supportive and reliable. They are excellent team players, but they are risk-averse and may tolerate an unpleasant environment rather than risk a change.

When working with Nurturers, make sure to:

- Behave honestly, sincerely, and attentively
- Allow time for them to open up to you
- Show how your solution will stabilize, simplify, or support
- Stay in touch . . . keep things running smoothly
- Try not to rush them, but do provide gentle, helpful nudges to help them decide

EXAMINER

Definition: A person who inspects or analyzes a person, place, or thing in detail, while testing their knowledge or skill by asking questions.

Examiners tend to be very thorough, efficient, task-driven people. They seek information and knowledge and love to check things off their "to-do" list. Because Examiners need a lot of information, they tend to make decisions more slowly than the Go-Getters and Promoters. They have a propensity toward perfectionism. Examiners tend to be very good conversationalists as they know a lot about a lot of topics. They attend networking functions only to market their business, and once they achieve their goal for the evening, they usually leave the event as quickly as possible.

Examiners are always in control of their emotions (note the poker-faces of many *Jeopardy!* contestants) and may become uncomfortable around people who are less self-contained (i.e., emotional and bubbly like Promoters). They tend to see the serious, complex side of situations. Their intelligence and natural wit, however, gives them unique, quick, and off-the-wall senses of humor.

When working with Examiners, make sure to:

- Avoid small talk, except to initially establish your credibility
- Ask relevant, fact-oriented questions
- Back up your talk with evidence
- Stress what your company does better than your competition in a factual way
- Seek specific feedback on your product/service performance

THE BOTTOM LINE

Once you start to understand these four different behavioral styles, networking in general and building your business in particular becomes a whole lot easier.

Why?

Because instead of "hitting it off" with some, and not with others, you'll have the tools to easily identify someone, adapt to their style, help them feel comfortable—and make them feel good at the same time!

And in an economy where relationships truly are the currency of today's business professional, you'll be well on your way toward making those connections while networking like a pro!

If you'd like to dig deeper into this material, check out the book *Room Full of Referrals* by Tony Alessandra, Ivan Misner, and Dawn Lyons (Paradigm Publishing, 2012).

18

Where Do I Start?

I f you've never before attended a networking event, you may be a little nervous about your first time. That's only natural. The room will be full of people who will be mostly strangers to you, and you'll notice right away that most of them will seem to know other attendees—some of them will seem to be acquainted with everybody!—and will be engaged in lively conversations. Unless you're the most gregarious person on the planet, you'll have some butterflies at the idea of going in and meeting all these new people.

Although it's natural to be nervous, be reassured that it would be hard to find a more open, inviting group of people than a gathering of business networkers. These are men and women who delight in meeting new people and welcoming them into their networks. Most are just naturally interested in people, and every new face represents a potential new relationship as well as a richer personal, social, and business experience down the line.

When you go to a mixer or other informal gathering, your first glimpse of the room may be daunting. You'll be confronted with a room full of strangers busily involved in conversations. If you were a fly on the chandelier, you might see something like the scenario in Figure 18.1.

Figure 18.1
Networking Mixer

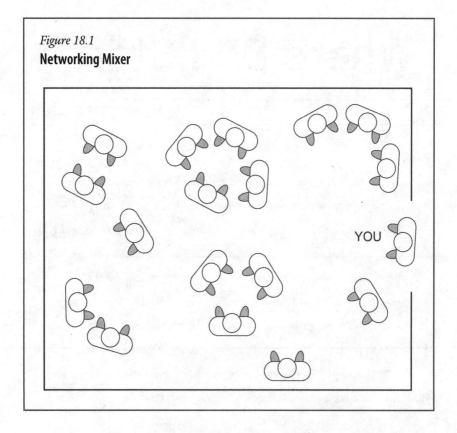

You can see in Figure 18.1 that conversations are going on in clusters of two, three, four, or more people. As a stranger, you may feel that if you try to join any of the clusters, you will be intruding. It's an awkward moment, and you may not know quite what to do or where to start.

If you take a closer look, though, the clusters are different and not just in the number of people in them. The way the groups are configured can tell you a lot about how you will be received if you approach them. Notice, for instance, that some of the groups are configured like those in Figure 18.2.

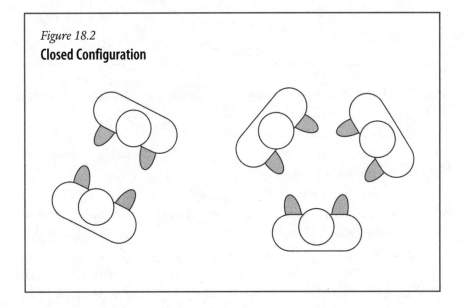

Figure 18.2
Closed Configuration

The people in the Figure 18.2 group, a closed two and a closed three, are facing inward, away from the rest of the room. They are engaged in private conversations. No matter which direction you approach from, their backs are turned to you. These groups are closed, at least for the moment. Unless you like awkward pauses or hostile glares, don't try to force yourself in.

Other clusters look more like those in Figure 18.3 on page 126.

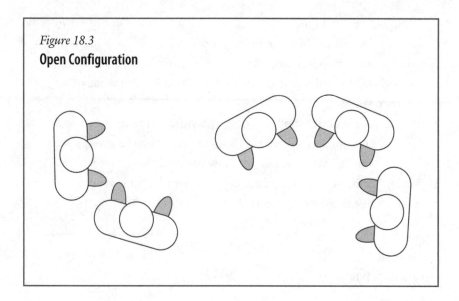

Figure 18.3
Open Configuration

These groups, exemplified here by an open two and an open three, have left an open side from which you can approach them face to face. This orientation is a welcoming configuration; it signals that their conversation is not private and that you would be welcome to join them and introduce yourself.

If you watch for a few minutes, you'll see groups open and close; this is an outward sign of the ebb and flow of the conversation. When a closed group opens, it means there is a break in the intensity of the conversation, or at least in its privacy. Some of the participants may be looking around the room, getting ready either to move or to accept new people into the cluster. That's a good time to join because it often means the conversation has slowed down or come to a halt and they're ready for a fresh topic—or a fresh face.

As you enter the room, here's what your awareness of these cluster dynamics should be telling you (refer to Figure 18.4 on page 127). Groups that are closed, like A, B, and C, are probably engaged in private conversations and are not good places to introduce yourself at the moment. Person F, who entered the room just ahead of you, is heading straight for Person G, who apparently knows him. They

Figure 18.4
Networking Mixer

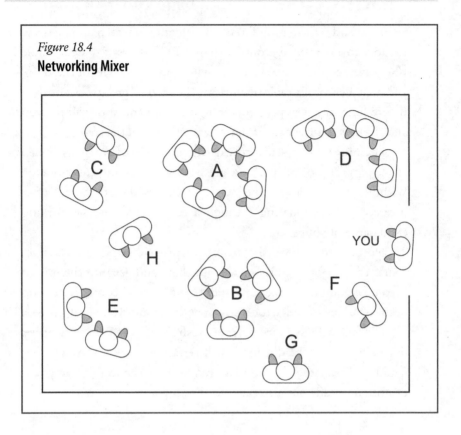

probably have some things to say to each other. Don't join them immediately; wait until you see whether they form an open two or a closed two.

Groups that have an open side, like D and E, are implicitly welcoming you to join them. Slide in and listen for a while until you can unobtrusively join the conversation. The others will probably smile and introduce themselves, and you will have started the process of making new friends. Person H, on the other hand, seems to be standing by himself for the moment; this might be a good opportunity to walk up and immediately introduce yourself.

Some of the people who attend a mixer stay grouped together for the entire event. However, if you watch these fixed groups closely, you will see that they open and close from time to time. Other groups break up and reform in different combinations. Watch and be ready to move to a new open group or to introduce yourself to new people who join the group you're in. You will soon get the feel of the room and will be comfortable navigating from one group to another. Before long, the new person coming through the door will see you and think you are the most popular networker in the room.

Learning how to read a crowd, whatever its size, and gauge when to join a group of people who are networking is an acquired skill. Without it, you might find such gatherings daunting and, after unsuccessfully wandering through a few, decide that networking events are not your game.

Nothing could be further from the truth. Networking is a contact sport. You've got to put yourself out there and get into the mix to become a good networker. In order to make those connections, you need to be able to gauge the warmth of the groups you see at a mixer.

It's still a long journey from fresh face to master networker, but being able to read a room will certainly get you through that daunting first meeting. You may even find it so enjoyable that you'll be not only ready but also eager to show up at the next one.

19

The 12 x 12 x 12 Rule

Perception is reality.

How many times have you heard that saying? Probably enough to know that the way you're perceived really does affect the business you conduct (or don't conduct) with other people. This is especially true when it comes to networking and meeting someone for the first time, and this is where the 12 x 12 x 12 rule becomes so important.

What exactly is the 12 x 12 x 12 rule? Basically, it involves three questions:

1. How do you look from 12 feet away? Do you look the part?
2. How do you come across from 12 inches away? Does your attitude and body language reflect what they first saw?
3. What are the first 12 words out of your mouth?

What we're talking about is perception versus reality and how important it is to create the right perception of yourself and your business.

Let's face it: as a businessperson, you've got a lot going on. There are people to see, places to go, and a whole lot of stuff to do. Can you do all this and look and act presentable at all times, too? Quite frankly, it can be a little overwhelming for even the sanest of people.

To complicate things further, most prospects don't care how much you've got going on or how many balls you have in the air. They just want to know if you're a potential solution to a problem they have, and their initial perception of you goes a long way in making that determination.

The same is true for potential referral partners.

They want to know if they can trust you with their referrals—people (and sometimes clients) with whom they have a good relationship. Do you have your act together so you won't jeopardize their good name when they refer business to you? Right or wrong, their initial perception of you is going to play a large part in answering that question.

This is precisely what the 12 x 12 x 12 rule is all about. It looks at you from the perspective of other people (prospects or referral partners) and shows you how to optimize their perception.

This does not mean manipulating or deceiving them; experienced people can see through that. Nor is it about checking your personality at the door. What it does mean is fine-tuning your networking practices to avoid shooting yourself in the foot. It's a lot like investing in a new wardrobe to spruce up your image.

That said, let's go over the specifics of the 12 x 12 x 12 rule and how you can manage the perception others have of you.

LOOK THE PART BEFORE GOING TO THE EVENT
(HOW DO YOU LOOK FROM 12 FEET AWAY?)

You'd be surprised how many people fall short in the fundamental area of appearance. If it's a chamber of commerce networking breakfast, don't go casual. Instead, consider wearing a good suit or nice outfit. You need to be well rested and clearheaded when attending a morning networking session; make a conscious effort to get plenty of sleep the night before. If you're not a morning person, hit the sack earlier than usual so you don't look like the walking dead. Regardless of how many cups of coffee you've had, people can tell if you're not all there.

MAKE SURE YOUR BODY LANGUAGE SENDS THE RIGHT MESSAGE
(HOW DO YOU COME ACROSS FROM 12 INCHES AWAY?)

When it comes to forming networking relationships, most of the important information—trustworthiness, friendliness, sincerity, openness—is communicated through nonverbal cues such as posture, facial expression, and hand gestures. When engaging in conversation, look the other person directly in the eye and stay focused on what he's saying. (With a lot of hustle and bustle going on, this can be harder than it sounds.) Lean a bit into the conversation rather than away from it; don't stand rigid with your arms crossed.

Attitude Is Everything!

When meeting someone for the first time, a lot can be said about how much your attitude can impact her first impression. In our survey to determine what others perceive as the most important characteristics of a great networker, having a positive attitude was only bested by being a good listener. So make sure that when you're talking to others, you have a positive, upbeat attitude.

BRIAN

For me, I'll sometimes make a positive comment on a tie or a nice shirt someone is wearing. Or I'll talk about how much I'm really enjoying the event or the food. Heck, I'll even talk about the weather if appropriate!

The point: Make sure to be upbeat and energetic—the type of person that others want to spend time with.

GET YOUR ACT TOGETHER

Another part of the second "12 inches" away rule is making sure you know which pocket your business cards are in and having plenty on hand. Nothing screams, "One of these days I've got to get organized!" louder than handing a potential referral partner someone else's card. For the ladies, since you might not have pockets as readily available as your male counterparts, consider putting them in your purse, cell phone holder, or in a physical calendar/planner that you might carry with you.

Just make sure that you have some type of system for keeping your cards separate from the cards you receive at the event.

One more thing: remember to smile when meeting someone for the first time. Studies have shown that if you smile when you talk, you seem more open and forthright. Obviously, you don't want to go overboard with this and start grinning and shaking hands like a hyperactive clown; just show that you're having a good time, and that will send the right message.

BRIAN

At one event a few years ago, a man handed me every business card he had but his own. He looked in his left pocket, his right pocket, his coat pocket, and everywhere else, but all he could come up with was other people's business cards. (There were other people waiting for his card as well.) I began to feel sorry for him; you could see his credibility dropping like a stone. Unfortunately, every networking event has someone like that, and believe me, you don't want to be that person.

HAVE THE FIRST 12 WORDS READY TO ROLL OFF YOUR TONGUE (WHAT ARE THE FIRST 12 WORDS OUT OF YOUR MOUTH?)

When someone asks you what you do, make sure you're ready with a response that is succinct but memorable. You can refer to Chapter 23: Telling Your Company's Story for our formula on constructing a solid USP. As a reminder, the USP should tell listeners what you do in a manner that gets them to ask "how" you do it.

We like to think of a good USP as the offline equivalent of a good post on social media . . . something that promotes curiosity and engagement. Remember, the attention span of the average adult is 20 seconds; a long, drawn-out answer to the question isn't going to work.

A USP is obviously something you'll have to tailor to your specific business, but can you see how it packs more punch than just telling people you're a consultant? Whatever 12 or 20 words you choose, make sure your answer is quick and informative without sounding over-rehearsed or contrived.

Sometimes, people ask us what part the 12 x 12 x 12 rule plays in formulating your elevator pitch, and it has to do with the first 12 words out of your mouth—your unique selling proposition. (Just as a reminder, your elevator pitch is made up of three to five sentences telling people what you do and how you do it. This is the 30-second or 60-second "commercial" you sometimes hear at networking events. Your unique selling proposition is not only part of the elevator pitch but it's also answering the specific question, "What do you do?" that so many people ask at networking events. Your unique selling proposition is a standalone entity on some occasions, while part of your overall pitch on other occasions when you have more time.) Those 12 words form the initial sentence of your elevator pitch are designed to get people's attention. From there, we suggest using language that tells a story or makes a point.

BRIAN

My USP and elevator pitch are real easy.

"Hi, my name is Brian Hilliard, and I help busy entrepreneurs market their business in less than 90 days. A lot of times, I run into people who are good at what they're good at but not so great at letting others know. What I do is create a tight, easy-to-implement marketing plan that even the busiest of people can use right away."

That is good for about 30 seconds, and depending on how much time I have, I can go into a specific story or situation that describes me affecting that result with my clients.

Now for the record, just because it says "elevator pitch" doesn't necessarily mean that it needs to be as long as an elevator ride.

Meaning 30 seconds is totally acceptable as long as it conveys your point.

Perception is reality when it comes to meeting people for the first time. If people perceive you as not being right for them, they simply won't be inclined to refer business to you, regardless of the work you can actually do. However, by keeping the 12 x 12 x 12 rule in mind, you'll go a long way toward creating the right impression in the blink of an eye.

20

Three Questions to Determine the "Right" Networking Event for You

Up to this point, we've talked about networking in terms of its general principles and the mindset you need to have to make it work, but now we want to shift gears and talk about developing a strategy that can help you jump into networking with both feet—or to put it another way, to create a framework that will help you decide which events you should attend and which you should pass over.

After all, let's face it, in most major cities, you can attend eight to ten networking events on any given day. Assuming that your minimum time investment is two hours per event (this takes into account getting in the car, driving downtown, parking, and participating in the event), it's easy to see how this networking thing can be a full-time job.

So the question becomes this: how can a time-strapped businessperson figure out which networking events she should attend and which she should let go by the wayside? The answer: by developing a networking strategy.

Most successful companies have a business plan that coordinates the many facets of that enterprise into a coherent document. These companies usually have a marketing plan as well that includes a month-by-month set of actions for getting the word out about the business.

CREATE YOUR PLAN

Why not have a networking strategy that helps you plan which events to attend? Here are three easy—but definitely essential—questions you need to answer in order to create a plan that will work for you.

1. Who Are My Best Prospects?

The first question is another way of asking, "What is my target market?" You'd be surprised at the number of business professionals who can't define their target market. Most of them either reply, "Everyone!" or offer some vague description that sounds good at first but offers little in the way of useful specifics. This is why business professionals so often find themselves running all over town, trying to attend every networking event that comes down the pike. As the George Harrison song says, "If you don't know where you're going, any road will get you there." Since they don't have time to follow up immediately with most of the people they meet, they often don't get as much business as they'd like; then they throw their hands in the air and wail, "Networking doesn't work for me!"

But as a smart, enterprising businessperson, you already know that networking works. It's just a matter of developing a strategy that puts you into contact with the right people.

The right people? If you're not sure who those folks might be for your business, go back and take a look at your list of past clients. What industries were they in? How long had they been in business? Were your clients even businesses to begin with, or have you worked mostly with consumers?

As an example, if you're a real estate agent, you might want to meet first-time home buyers and people who are interested in moving downtown. If you're a management consultant, your target audience might be representatives from companies in a specific industry (for instance, medical) or with annual sales greater than a certain figure (say $1 million). Or, if you're an accountant or a CPA, you might be targeting small-business owners—one- or two-person shops that don't have the resources to hire a full-time bookkeeper.

Each one of those is fine, but each target market will have a strategy that requires you to network in different places. Once you've put together a profile of the people you've worked with in the past, pick up the phone and run it by a few trusted friends and colleagues. See what they think. People who are close to you often have insights into patterns that you tend to overlook because you're busy with day-to-day operations, and this is a great time to get their input on who they feel would be a good fit for your business. Once you get that nailed down, you can go on to the next question.

2. Where Can I Meet My Best Prospects?

Networking doesn't mean just hopping into the car and attending the next chamber of commerce event. Yes, the chamber and other business associations are excellent means of finding and meeting new prospects, and we recommend them to anyone as a good starting point. But as your business evolves and you begin targeting specific niche markets, there are other venues and opportunities that fall outside the typical networking event—and that's the kind of out-of-the-box thinking we're going to discuss here.

Generally speaking, if you're trying to meet more small-business owners, you should spend time at the chamber of commerce, your local business association, or a referral group. Not only do these groups have exactly the type of audience you want to meet, but with referral groups, and BNI in particular, there's a system in place that will help you help others get more referrals for you.

If you're looking to meet representatives from bigger corporations in your area, we recommend service clubs, nonprofit groups, and volunteer work. Another good way to come into contact with those folks is through homeowners associations, most of which meet at least once a month. It's a great way to get in contact with folks who are in corporations but don't attend typical networking events.

If your business is geared more toward consumers, then getting involved with your kids' events—Little League, Boy Scouts, and so forth—is another good way to meet the right people.

If you're that real estate agent who wants to meet first-time home buyers and people interested in moving downtown, you'll probably find more prospects by networking at downtown events. It doesn't matter which event, as long as it's being held in the city center. That should bring you into contact with people who might be thinking about moving out of their apartment and getting into a house. Look also for networking events likely to be attended by young professionals, since these are the people most likely to be living in an apartment while accumulating the disposable income to buy a downtown condo or home.

For the management consultant who wants to meet people in million-dollar companies, we'd recommend networking at service clubs or nonprofit groups. Why? Because the directors and CEOs of large companies are less likely to be at your local chamber's after-hours event than in a civic organization like Habitat for Humanity, Kiwanis International, or Rotary International. We also recommend trying to get on your service club's board or leadership team; that way you're interfacing with more of the movers and shakers of your community. Careful, though: if you're too direct in these clubs, too obviously looking for business relationships, you won't be welcomed. These groups are more civic than business oriented, which means you'll have to establish your credibility through community-oriented activities rather than business deals.

3. Whom, Exactly, Do I Want to Meet?

You've heard the assertion that there are six degrees of separation between you and any other person, haven't you? The idea is that, through at most five intermediaries, you can meet anybody on the planet that you choose to. It's a networker's dream of heaven.

The trouble is it just isn't true.

In their book, *The 29% Solution: 52 Weekly Networking Success Strategies* (Greenleaf Book Group, 2008), Ivan Misner and Michelle Donovan point out that the "six degrees of separation" notion applies to only a small fraction of the population at most. Experiments by sociologist Stanley Milgram in the 1960s and '70s found that, yes, the people who made the desired connection did it through an average of five or six people, but some did it through two connections while others took ten intermediaries or more. But here's the real hitch: only 29 percent were successful in making the connection at all. The overwhelming majority (71 percent) never got through to the intended person! Worse, other studies by Milgram achieved an even more anemic rate of success.

This tells us that most people are not well connected in any practical sense. However, among people who are extraordinarily well connected, you can get in contact with anyone through, on the average, only five intermediaries. The best networkers strive to be among that 29 percent, and our work is to help people join this world of master networkers.

Now, here's an interesting fact that we've noticed: even accomplished networkers sometimes fail to realize that they're closer to a much-desired contact than they imagine. There's a story about two networkers who had worked together closely for many years. One day one of them said to the other, "You know, I've been going to a lot of events lately, but I still haven't been able to meet one guy I really need to see. If I could meet the CEO of LotsaBucks Corporation, I could take it easy for a while. But there's no way I'm going to get a meeting with him by calling."

"There's a trade show next month. Come with me, and I'll introduce you."

"You know this guy?"

"Yeah, we've been in the same country club for seven years."

"Why didn't you tell me you knew him?"

"You didn't ask."

The principles behind making this kind of connection—summed up in the simple aphorism "You don't know whom they know"—are ably outlined by Wayne Baker at Humax in a referral tool he calls the Reciprocity Ring. Boiled down to its essentials, the idea is that the greater the number of networks you're connected with, the greater the chance that there's a short chain of contacts between you and anyone you'd care to name. All you have to do is recognize that fact and ask a few people a specific question or two. The answers will either put you in direct contact or lead you in the direction of the networking events you need to attend.

Even if you can't name the people you want to meet, the better you can describe them, the greater the chance that you'll get to meet your ideal contact. The secret ingredient in this principle is specificity. The way to meet the unknown contact is to be as specific as possible without closing out all possible variations. You can do this by starting your question like this: "Whom do you know who . . . ?" You complete the sentence with specifics: "Whom do you know who is a new parent?" "Whom do you know who belongs to an organization that builds houses for the homeless?" By asking for a specific kind of contact, you focus the other person's attention on details that are more likely to remind him of a specific person than if you asked, "Do you know anyone who needs my services?"

Now, before we paint too rosy a picture on meeting the right people, let us be clear on one thing: senior executives are hiding from you.

Well, maybe not hiding, but you can't expect the director of marketing at a Fortune 1000 company to go out of his way to meet

IVAN

The VCP Process® is part of the foundation of relationship networking. You start by being visible—that is, by being at networking events and getting acquainted with a potential referral partner. Credibility comes after you've had dealings with the person and become known to him as someone who does good work and can be trusted. Profitability comes last, after you and your networking partner have established a history of helping each other succeed in business.

Depending on the frequency and quality of your contacts and the desire of both of you to develop the relationship, it may take months or even years to progress through these phases, but the payoff is well worth the investment. This simple concept has made a bigger difference in more people's networking efforts than any other single idea I've discussed. When people get this, all the techniques I teach fall into place much more effectively.

you. Don't worry, it's nothing personal. It's just that he's a very busy person, and it would be literally a full-time job to listen to every Tom, Dick, and Harriet who wants to sell him or his company on some new idea. That's why it's important to surround yourself with quality business contacts; since the best way to your ideal contact very often is through another contact.

It's less of "I'm going to this networking event to find the right prospect" and more of "I'm networking to develop mutually beneficial relationships with people in the local business community." It's recognition that the development of a mature, mutually beneficial referral relationship follows the VCP Process® through its three stages: visibility, credibility, and profitability.

One of the great things about the growth of referral marketing is that there are so many more opportunities available today than there were even five years ago. Unfortunately, there's also a downside: you may quickly feel overwhelmed by the vast number of events in your town and by the whirlwind of networking that seems to characterize most of them. However, when you answer these three key questions and begin creating a strategy, you'll find that the networking world truly is your oyster. All you have to do is put yourself in the ideal position for meeting the people who are most likely to do business with you.

21

Where's Your Attention Focused?

ave you ever wondered why most people are better at talking than listening? Or how sometimes when you're talking with someone you can tell that he's only half-listening to what you're saying? We realize this very well might irritate you. We realize this because, as you might recall, our survey of business professionals (see Chapter 14: Seven Characteristics of a Great Networker) ranked being a "good listener" as the number-one characteristic of great networkers. People like to be heard; more than anything else, people value a networker's ability to listen.

So if you hope and expect to get more business while networking, then pay special attention to the fact that effective professional networkers have mastered the skill of listening.

Fact: The human brain can think at 400 to 450 words per minute; the average person, however, speaks 100 to 150 wpm.

Let's say you're at a networking event, and you're in a conversation with someone who speaks rapidly—maybe somewhere in the neighborhood of 150 wpm. While that person is talking, your brain is processing at a rate of 400 wpm. So, if you're thinking at 400 and the person you're talking to is speaking at 150, then what you do with that extra 250 wpm capacity is going to determine how good a listener you are.

Focused attention means concentrating 100 percent of your attention on the message the other person is communicating.

Where is your attention focused? Are you planning your response while the other person is talking, or are you considering her point and taking mental notes? Are you scanning the room, trying to find the next person to meet, or are you devoting your full attention to this individual?

The reason some people aren't very good listeners is because during most conversations they're spending that extra thinking capacity on something other than the conversation at hand. And in today's email-typing, screen-scrolling, voice mail-checking world, where multitasking is very much the standard operating procedure, everyone seems to be doing two or three things at once.

Recommendation: At your next networking event, shut off your multitasking gene. Make it a point to block out everyone else in the room and focus your attention on the discussion at hand.

You might argue that not every person you meet will be an immediate prospect for your business. Yes, time is money, and conventional wisdom tells us that you shouldn't be wasting your time with just one person. But here's the thing: even if the one person you're devoting attention to isn't an immediate prospect, you never know whom he might know (Referral! Referral!).

In any event, the last thing you want to do when networking is to seem preoccupied with finding a more important person to talk to. If you've ever been on the other side of that conversation, engaged with someone whose gaze, you began to realize, was focused somewhere over your shoulder like a searchlight, you'll know what we mean when we say that a good swift referral was not the first thing you were thinking about giving that person.

Here's how to avoid being that searchlight networker: before each event, think of a few questions you'd like to ask each new contact—just two or three questions that will get the other person talking about a subject that might be of interest you. For instance, most of us are interested in hearing how people get new business. Not only can asking questions provide some fresh, new ideas that we might use, but it also creates an opportunity to add value to the conversation by bringing up a point the other person might not have considered. If you're a PR consultant, you might want to ask how your new contact leverages local print and radio media to get more exposure for her business. It's an area you presumably know a lot about and talking about it gives you an opportunity to gain credibility. If you play your cards right, this person might even turn out to be someone who ultimately contracts your services. However, that will happen only if you take the time to listen closely and understand. Focused attention is essential to doing that.

A friend of ours told us about a person who went a step further and actually used focused attention all the time, not just during networking events. Whenever someone walked into his office, he physically cleared whatever documents he had on his desk and focused all his attention on that person. No cell phones ringing, no emails popping up—just him and that other person. Wow! Now that sends a powerful message.

Imagine being able to send that message to everyone in your professional life. How much of an impact would that have on your ability to get more referrals?

Standout Questions

Advance bonus question: what's the easiest way to be seen as a bore?

That's right. Talk about yourself.

So why would anyone think that successful networking means cornering as many people as possible and telling them all about your business? To the contrary, the best way to entertain a new contact and potential future referral partner is to get him to talk about himself and his business.

Your goal in a networking event is to make yourself memorable without talking about yourself. It sounds paradoxical, doesn't it? But if you know how to do it, you will stand out in people's minds when they look back on the event. The secret is simply to ask people questions about themselves and their businesses.

A lot of people you run into at networking events are so busy talking about themselves, their products, and all the great things they can do for you that they never take a breath and ask about you. (These are often the same people who say networking doesn't work for them.) Instead of competing with these folks by getting into a boasting contest about who does the most business, imagine the result of asking questions that encourage them to freely share that information. Now, instead of them talking and you interrupting (or vice versa), you are creating a networking environment in which they're talking, you're listening, and everyone is feeling heard. Not only will this technique help you stand out from the crowd, but it will also get you a ton of referrals.

People refer business to people they like and respect. This is why, when you give others time to tell their story and explain their business, your stock automatically rises in their eyes. Throw in that you've got a top-flight product or service—don't worry, eventually the other guy will wind down and you'll get to talk about yourself—and you'll see how it's a lot easier than many people think to create a solid referral partner.

QUESTION TIME

It all begins with your first conversation. If you lead off by asking the right questions—questions that demonstrate a genuine interest in the other person's business—you cultivate an attitude of trust and rapport from the start. By "right questions," we do not mean prospecting or qualifying questions, the kind you would ask if you were trying to size up the other person's potential for helping you or to grab some business right off the bat. Those should never be the goal of the first conversation.

Following are five good questions to ask that will make you a standout.

"What Do You Like Best about What You Do?"

If you've been out networking before, you already know that "What do you do?" is one of the first questions people ask you. This isn't necessarily a bad thing, but it doesn't leave you much room to maneuver after both you and your fellow networker have answered the question for each other:

"So what do you do?"

"I'm a public relations consultant. How about you?"

"I see. Well, I own a print shop."

(Awkward four-second pause that seems to go on forever.)

Look how much better it works if you follow up with our question:

"Oh, a print shop. That's interesting. What do you like best about the printing business?"

This leads to more interesting conversation about the other person's business, his likes and dislikes, his experience, and so forth. It makes the conversation flow and lets you relax while you learn about his trade or profession.

What's more, if he's like most of us, he will eventually decide he's talked enough and will ask you the same question—what do you like best about your business? Be ready with a good response:

Well, to be honest with you, I really enjoy helping clients get the word out about their business in ways they might not have thought about. Often, when people hear "public relations," their first thought is of a big Madison Avenue office—and huge retainer fees.

But that's not how we operate. We help business professionals get more business through print and radio media without it costing them an arm and a leg. I can't tell you how satisfying that is.

A response like this answers the question, raises some important issues, and explains how you're different from others in the industry. If the other person is thinking about using a PR firm or knows someone else who might need one, then you've gone a long way toward setting the stage for a possible referral.

"You Mentioned That You Were in [Industry]. What Got You Started in That Direction?"

This question is much like the previous one in that it gives the other person a chance to talk about personal goals and desires and to look favorably on you for asking it. It also gives you insight into how dedicated she is to her profession and how proficient she may be at it. When you learn what her previous experience has been, you will begin to see ways that you might refer other people to her for specialized products or services.

"Where Else Do You Usually Network?"

Amy Windham, a colleague of Brian's in Atlanta, first brought this one to our attention, and it's an absolute gem. Not only does it help break the ice during that sometimes awkward period just after you've introduced yourself, but it also gives you a chance to talk about something you both know a little bit about.

Another reason we like this question is because it gives you the opportunity to make an instant connection. How? It provides the other person valuable information he didn't previously have, on a topic that's relevant to him. As we all know, a great step toward creating a solid referral partner is to first make a connection with that person.

This is an example of why we believe asking the right questions makes you stand out from the crowd. A conversation might start with "Where else do you normally network?" and that dovetails into an extended conversation about the other person's business. Within the first few minutes, the person you are speaking with will likely be listening with interest and thinking of ways to help. This is all you can ask for when meeting someone for the first time.

"What Are Some of Your Biggest Challenges?"

This is a great question that can be used toward the end of the conversation. Of the four questions we've talked about, this usually

BRIAN

I was at a networking event one morning when I asked a gentleman where else he usually networked. He said that he didn't know of any other networking events around town since he had just moved to Atlanta.

As a person who likes to consider himself a connoisseur of local networking events, I found that to be music to my ears. I asked him what kind of prospects he was trying to meet—large corporations, small businesses, or something in between. I wanted to get a feel for the types of events that might work for him.

The man replied that his business focused on the technology sector and that he would love to meet anyone in that field. I assured him that this would not be a problem and mentioned the names of a couple of groups I thought could help. You could see the relief in his eyes. He was genuinely grateful that someone was willing to help him out with some business-generating information.

elicits the longest response. Why? Because you're asking about her reasons, her passion, and her motivation for being in her specific business in the first place. We've had people tell us all sorts of things when we've asked this question.

"How Can I Help You?"

If you've asked a new acquaintance some or all of the previous questions, the conversation has gone well, and you've decided this person is someone you'd like to have in your business network, this is a good question to ask. His answer may tell you something that will enable you to help him, and being helpful is the best way to start building a solid relationship. To a networker who is living the principle of Givers Gain, it's a question that comes naturally because that networker is one who has adopted the mindset of giving value and service to others without any thought of immediate return. It demonstrates that you have the other person's interests uppermost in your mind, and it's an excellent way to build the credibility and trust you'll want to share with a valuable networking partner.

Remember, everyone has a story. Make it your job to find out what it is.

THE ANSWERS YOU WANT

Asking the right questions is about earning trust and gaining rapport with your new contact. It's about your contact feeling comfortable telling you about her business without competing with you for airtime. But most of all, asking the right questions is about developing a relationship with a future referral partner so she'll be more than happy to give you any referral that might come her way.

23

Telling Your Company's Story

It's not all about the other person, you know. After you've asked your new acquaintance all the right questions and laid the foundation for a cordial business relationship, the conversation will eventually turn to you and with any luck you'll find yourself answering many of the same questions you just asked. This is an important part of the give-and-take, and you should be prepared for it. After all, others have to know your business if you're going to get any.

There are two kinds of audiences that need to hear your company's story. One is the people you interact with directly while networking. These could be people you meet and exchange pleasantries with at a chamber of commerce mixer or, more to the point for a networking pro, one or more people in a dedicated referral networking group such as BNI; these are the folks you hope to turn into reliable sources of referrals. The other audience is people you don't meet, at least not right away, but who are told about you by your networking partner or referral source; they are your prospective customers.

YOUR UNIQUE SELLING PROPOSITION

One of the biggest mental hurdles businesspeople have is the idea that word-of-mouth marketing is about telling everyone they see everything they do and that getting more referrals is simply a matter of talking to more people. But that's not the case at all. In getting your message across, less is more. The trick is to come up with a succinct, memorable unique selling proposition (USP) that you can use at all your networking events.

Your USP is basically a brief description of the purpose of your business, stated in the most succinct and compelling way possible in order to get others to understand the unique value of what you do. A good USP simply tells people what you do, in a manner that gets them to ask how you do it:

- "We work with business owners to help them handle the two biggest challenges they face on a day-to-day basis." —Mike Miller, commercial insurance agent
- "I help nonprofit organizations connect with their community through the game of golf." —John Parker, golf fundraising specialist
- "I work with municipalities on capital improvement projects in the areas of water, wastewater, and drainage." —Sharmaine James, project engineer in New Orleans
- "I work with bright, successful, family-oriented business owners who are so busy on the immediate that they lose sight

of the fundamentals that can affect their family's financial well-being." —Andrew Rodgers, financial advisor

- "I help business owners answer the three most important questions as it relates to their family and the preservation of their business." —Victor Banks, financial advisor

- "I teach people how to create Referrals for Life®." —Ivan Misner, Ph.D., founder of BNI and co-founder of Asentiv

Notice that these USPs are short, sweet, and straight to the point. Your USP tells people the type of client you work with and the benefit you provide. If you meet someone while networking who fits your target market, then her next question should be "How do you do that?" And off you'll go talking about your business.

This is why having a good USP is important. It describes your business in terms of the needs it can fill and allows people to decide whether they want to learn more. Instead of requiring you to identify and approach target markets, it lets your target market self-select.

Let's say you're the proprietor of a preschool day-care center. At a local networking event, you meet a man who is single. What's the likelihood he's going to want to hear your message? Slim to none. It has nothing to do with you; it's just that he's not a candidate for your services, so why waste your time and effort on him?

But then suppose this man is recently divorced and, unbeknownst to you, has custody of his children. He might want to learn more about your business—if you've crafted your USP to catch his interest.

Here's how to create your own USP:

- Focus on two or three profitable target markets for your business—groups of people for whom your services are best suited. For the day-care example, one of your target markets might be families with children ages one to five and who live within 15 miles of your business.

- Identify some challenges facing your target market. If you own a restaurant that caters to tourists, one of their likely concerns is finding a good meal at a good price. While traveling, you've probably asked a desk clerk yourself to recommend a good Chinese or Italian restaurant. As a restaurateur, you can address this challenge by getting to know all the hotel staff within five to seven miles of your establishment. Chat with them, bring them some samples, and put together a menu and free-appetizer coupons that they can hand out to arriving guests. If they know you've got the goods, they'll recommend you with confidence.
- Create a snappy one- or two-sentence USP: "I help [target market] [solve problem]." As you saw from the previous examples and in Chapter 16: Top Five Most Common Networking Mistakes, that's pretty much the format we used.

Don't confuse a USP with a memory hook. There are some similarities, but a memory hook has a distinctive twist to it that makes it linger in the listener's mind like a catchy melody. If you are in a strong-contact networking group, you know that a memory hook is best used during your 60-second chapter presentation as way of getting members of the group to remember who you are and what products or services you provide.

A memory hook is short and catchy, often using rhyme or wordplay. Here's an example, a great memory hook used by a dentist in California: "I believe in the tooth, the whole tooth, and nothing but the tooth, so help me God." Used to kick off or wrap up a presentation to a large group, it's great at helping people remember who he is and what he does. However, most people would probably edge away from him if he used his memory hook face-to-face at a networking event:

Prospect: "So, what do you do?"
Stan: "I believe in the tooth, the whole tooth . . ."

Prospect (backing away slowly): "Ohh-kaaay . . . ."

See how off that sounds? It just doesn't fit this situation. For a one-to-one conversation, a USP is better:

"I operate a dental practice. We specialize in prosthetic dentistry."

So if you're in a strong-contact networking group and have a memory hook but no USP, work on developing a good USP. If you have neither, you should start working on both. A memory hook is great on brochures, websites, fliers—even the back of your business card. Think of it as a tagline about your business that gets people to sit up and take notice.

Many people use their memory hooks week after week in a referral group. This is not only annoying but a waste of time. The USP is much more important in this setting. Your goal is to educate your referral partners, and a memory hook just won't do it. Use your memory hook only with groups of people who don't know you.

Regardless of your situation, developing a strong USP that your target market can quickly identify with will put you in great shape for attracting more referrals than you might think possible.

BRIEFING YOUR MESSENGER

Telling your company's story starts at your doorstep. You have to communicate what you do in a way that's clear to your referral sources. This is central to the referral marketing process for any networker because it teaches people how to send you referrals. People must know exactly what you do, what product or service you provide, how well you do it, and in what ways you're better at it than your competitors. You're responsible for communicating this information to your referral sources, and to communicate effectively, you must know your information inside and out.

It may seem like a no-brainer—don't we all know what we do for a living? Of course you do, but can you communicate it clearly and simply to your potential sources? If you think about it, you may find that you're not quite as clear as you thought you were. And if you can't tell your referral sources what you do or what you sell, how can they send you good referrals?

To ensure that your referral marketing campaign is as effective as possible, take a few minutes to get a clear picture of where your business stands today. You may think you know why you're in business, but perhaps it's been years since you've given it serious thought. Now is a good time to reexamine why you're doing what you're doing. Ask yourself the following questions, and write down your answers.

- Why am I in business?
- Why do I do what I do?
- How does my business serve others?
- What do I sell?
- Most important, what are the benefits—not the features—of my product or service?
- Who are my customers?
- What are my target markets? (Be specific; look at all the segments of your business to determine the niche, or niches, you prefer to work with.)
- What are my competencies, and what do I do best?
- How well do I compete?
- How do I stand out from my competition?

Answering these questions will help you tell others what your business is all about, and it will make you more effective at implementing a comprehensive referral program. After you've written down your answers, think about how you can effectively pass this information to your referral sources.

GETTING SPECIFIC

You're probably so accustomed to the ubiquitous "What do you do?" question at mixers, business events, and seminars that you hardly give a thought to how you're answering that question. It's not enough simply to tell your contacts your job description ("I own and operate a sporting goods store"). To deepen the relationship, you must talk about what you do in a way that, as Lou Cassara says, "communicates the magic of your vision expressed through your words." It should also be specific, should not use jargon, and should be stated in terms of benefits to the customer, not features. Say something along these lines: "I deal in sporting goods, and I specialize in team sports. I've outfitted most of the high school football teams in the district, and I can order custom-fitted shoulder pads and helmets for any player at a deep discount and have it delivered within five days. I also sponsor the local Pop Warner teams."

Now that's specific.

It also passes what author and speaker Sam Horn calls the "eyebrow test."

Sam says that when you give your USP to someone, listen to what they have to say but most importantly, watch for the reaction they have. She says that "if their eyebrows don't move, it means they're unmoved." If they're eyebrows scrunch down and furrow together—you've confused them. If however, their eyebrows go up, Sam says your USP has succeeded. "They're engaged, curious, and want to know more."

Too many business professionals and companies try to be all things to all people. Instead, try focusing on the things you do well and document those things and your vision in a way that you can communicate to others. By clearly understanding what you do, you'll be better able to communicate this to your referral partners, and this will help teach your referral sources whom they can refer to you. Ultimately, that's what networking is all about.

24

Quantity Is Fine, but Quality Is King

One of the biggest misconceptions we've seen about networking is the notion that it's an "all you can eat" affair. In other words, people go to an event, work the room in an effort to meet everyone there, and then judge their success by the number of cards they accumulate. Although we see a certain superficial logic in that, there's one fatal flaw with this kind of thinking: it assumes that the more people you meet at an event, the more successful your networking efforts are—and that's simply not the case.

Businesspeople unfamiliar with referral networking sometimes lose track of the fact that networking is the means—not the end—of their business-building activities. They attend three, four, or even five events in a week in a desperate grasp for new business. The predictable result is that they stay so busy meeting new people that they never have time to follow up and cultivate those relationships—and how can they expect to get that new business from someone

BRIAN

A few years back I found myself listening to someone brag about how successful he had been at networking that evening. He had met a bunch of new prospects and had a "stack of cards" right there in his pocket. His unspoken implication was that they just couldn't wait to buy his stuff later on. I was thinking, "OK, but how many of those folks feel that they know you and would be comfortable contracting your services, let alone referring you to their friends?"

I had been watching him "network" all evening. Take my word for it, he wasn't developing relationships. Sure, he shook their hands, told them all about his business, and "listened" for a few seconds. Then, whoosh! He was off to swap cards with the next poor sucker.

If you've ever run into anyone like that, you know that the last thing on your mind was giving him a referral. You simply didn't spend enough time with the guy. And even if you did, you probably didn't like the vibe you got while he was staring over your shoulder, looking at the person he wanted to talk to next.

When you're networking like a pro, you understand the importance of creating a visible identity and asking the right questions. You recognize the value of a unique selling proposition and how the 12 x 12 x 12 rule can manage the perception others have of you. Most important, you realize that meeting people at a networking event is merely the foundation upon which a future business relationship and its referrals are built. It's the start of the process—not the beginning, middle, and end of the story, the way our friend was viewing it.

they've only just met? As one of these unfortunates remarked to us, "I feel like I'm always doing business but rarely getting anything done."

IT'S ALL ABOUT THE RELATIONSHIPS

We certainly agree that meeting new people is an integral part of networking, but it's important to remember why we're doing it in the first place: to develop a professional rapport with individuals that will deepen over time into a trusting relationship that will eventually lead to a mutually beneficial and continuous exchange of referrals.

When meeting someone for the first time, focus on the potential relationship you might form. As hard as it may be to suppress your business reflexes, at this stage you cannot make it your goal to sell your services or promote your company. You're there to get to know a new person. A friend of ours told us something his dad always said: "You don't have to sell to friends." That's especially good advice when interacting with new contacts.

This certainly doesn't mean you'll never get to sell anything to people you meet while networking; it does, however, mean that you'll

IVAN

One of my company's directors struck up a conversation with a business owner at a networking function. The business owner told the director, "I'm really good at networking. I've been doing it for a long, long time."

"So what's your secret?" asked our director.

"Well, a friend and I enter a room together," the business owner said. "We draw an imaginary line down the middle. She takes the left side; I take the right. We agree to meet at a certain time to see who has collected the most cards. The loser buys the other one lunch."

The director asked, "So what do you do with all those cards?"

"I enter them into my distribution list and begin to send them information about my services. I have all their information, so that makes them all good prospects, right?"

This is a classic example of an entrepreneur not understanding that networking isn't about simply gathering contact information and following up on it later. That's nothing more than glorified cold calling. It gives me the chills. I used to teach cold-calling techniques to businesspeople, and I did it enough to know that I didn't want to ever do it again. I've devoted my entire professional life to teaching the business community that there's a better way to build long-term business.

need to employ a different approach. Networking isn't about closing business or meeting hordes of new people; it's about developing relationships in which future business can be closed. Once you understand that and put it into practice, you'll notice a few things happening to your business.

First, you'll stand out from the crowd with everyone you meet. People often ask us how they can get business at an event when there are so many other people trying to do the same thing. We simply tell them to stand out from the crowd by doing things a bit differently. A good way to do that is by asking a new contact good questions and taking the time to listen to her answers. (A good question is one that gets the person talking about herself while helping you understand her business. It is not an opportunity for you to vet this person as a client.)

Good questions not only get the ball rolling but also take the pressure off you to carry the conversation; meeting new people can be hard enough without feeling you have to be the life of the party to do it. If you're not sure what kinds of questions to ask, go back and reread Chapter 22: Standout Questions, where we talk about them in more detail.

Another good reason for adopting this advanced networking approach is that it will differentiate you from the competition. This is especially vital for mortgage brokers, real estate agents, insurance agents, CPAs, financial planners, and others in highly competitive industries. You can't go to a networking event without running into at least one person in some of those fields.

When you're networking like a pro and treating new contacts as future referral partners, you'll absolutely blow away any competitors who will still feel compelled to meet as many people as they can. Why? Because when you call your contacts back, they'll actually remember who you are and will be willing to meet with you again. This is obviously a critical next step for securing more business.

MAXIMIZE YOUR EVENT STRATEGY

With all of that in mind, let's take a look at some specific steps you can take toward getting more business from your very next event.

Limit the Number of Contacts per Event

The most important thing is the quality of the contacts, which means the type of contact, the relevance to your business and interests, how good a connection you're making, and the individual involved. At a typical event, five to ten contacts might be all you can handle. This may not seem like a lot of contacts, but it's really more than enough when you're talking to the right people. If you attend two events per week, that's eight (or more) events a month, or 40 to 80 new contacts every 30 days. Continue to do that over the next couple of months—while following up with the people that you've met—and you'll soon have more than enough high-quality contacts to keep you busy.

Spend Five to Ten Minutes Talking and Listening to Each Person

Just because you're not handing out your business card to 1,001 people doesn't mean you should spend 20 minutes talking to just one individual. Invest a few minutes in getting to know each person. Make sure to ask for her business card. Then follow up with her after the event; this is where the heavy lifting takes place. Remember, all we're doing now is setting the stage for future business.

Many people ask us how to end a conversation. Don't overthink this. It's pretty easy to end a conversation in a friendly and polite way. Here are two things that we do:

1. Based on something she says, think of someone in the room that might be interested in talking to her. Let her know about the person in the room, walk her over, and make an introduction. Then say that you'll leave them to get to know one

another. It's a great way to end a conversation and, at the same time, be a connector.

2. If there's no one to introduce the person to, then thank her for the conversation, let her know that you hope your paths cross again and ask for a card. Conversation over.

On the second approach, it's important to be genuine. If you hope to never meet that person again, don't remark, "you hope your paths cross again." Instead, say something polite and professional and ask for their card. Asking for a card and offering thanks has almost always worked for us. Again, don't overthink this and do not apologize for ending the conversation. Whatever you do—do not say you have someone else to meet. That puts people off.

Write Notes on the Backs of People's Cards

Not only will writing notes help you remember what the other person said at an event, but it will also slow you down a bit so you won't be

IVAN

CAUTION! In some cultures, especially some Asian countries, people will take great offense if you write on their business cards. If you are in doubt, ask the person if it's all right: "Do you mind if I make a note on the back of your card to remind me to get back to you on that?" This will allow her to give you permission, if she wishes, and it demonstrates that you are interested in responding to her questions or comments. Then, be absolutely sure you do respond; don't let it slide.

running around trying to meet the next person. On the front of the card you can write the date and name of the event where you met the person; on the back, a few quick notes about the conversation or anything else of note. When you contact the person later, this will give you something to refer to.

To reiterate two key ideas when it comes to meeting new people:

- You're not interested in selling anything to the person you're just meeting; you want to find some way you can help her. You understand, of course, that what goes around comes around, usually in the form of referrals for your business.
- You want to create a visible identity with everyone you meet. A visible identity is the answer to this question: "How can I differentiate myself, in the mind of this other person, from the other five people she's already met?"

Keeping those two ideas in mind will give you a leg up when meeting new contacts. Using this simple Givers Gain approach, you'll see an uptick in the amount of new business and referrals you get while networking.

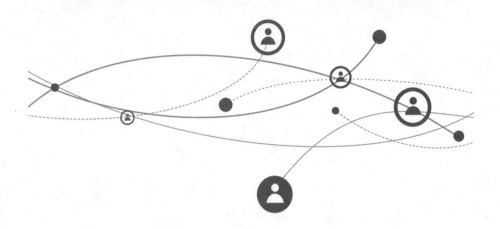

PART IV

MAKING YOUR NETWORK WORK

25

Getting More Referrals with a Formalized Referral Strategy

With referrals being the lifeblood of every business professional, people often ask us what single action they can take to generate more referral-based clientele. While we don't have a one-size-fits-all answer, creating a formalized referral strategy is a great start.

As the name implies, a formalized referral strategy is simply a structured, "locked down" process or strategy with the express purpose of deepening relationships and producing referrals.

While the specifics will vary depending on the business, it's something that any business can implement. Here are some of the components of a super-effective, easy-to-implement formalized referral strategy.

WRITE AN ONLINE NEWSLETTER

We find online newsletters to be highly effective, and many businesspeople include them in their formalized referral strategy. Remember, an online newsletter is simply an email that goes out once or twice a month to your network of contacts, clients, and referral partners.

The newsletter's content should be something of value to the readers. If you're a chiropractor, a newsletter that discusses health, nutrition, and exercises people can do to stay healthy would be appropriate. A photographer might consider publishing something about the subtleties—camera angle, lighting—of taking a good picture. (And with the multitude of the cell phones out there, and people taking pictures, who wouldn't want to learn information about that!) A career transition coach might have tips about interviewing, resume writing, and how people can find their next job.

The point is this: you want content that is both valuable to readers and potentially sharable to their friends. By providing useful content through an online, shareable method, you gain top-of-mind awareness (you're the first person people think of when they hear of your industry) among your network.

If you don't already have an online newsletter and are looking for a place to start, two of the more popular platforms are MailChimp and Constant Contact.

Both are easy to set up (even if you don't have a lot of technical skills) and can have you publishing your first newsletter in no time!

CREATE A POWER TEAM OF COMPLEMENTARY BUSINESSES

A power team is simply a collection of people you have a relationship with who operate complementary businesses or who cater to the same clientele. BNI chapters use this strategy regularly, but you can create a power team even if you're not a member of BNI. For example, a real estate power team could include a:

- Real estate agent
- Mortgage broker
- Property and casualty insurance agent
- Handyman
- Exterminator
- Closing attorney
- Home inspector

These are all people who "touch" a home purchase deal and who complement each other, meaning that if one finds a home buyer, then all of them benefit.

Weddings are another good power team opportunity. Assume you are one of the following professionals.

- Wedding planner
- Wedding photographer
- Hotel/venue owner or manager
- Caterer
- DJ/band
- Florist

You could get together every other week and pass referrals among each other. Forming a power team or plugging into one via a group like BNI can go a long way toward generating more referrals. We encourage you to consider creating a power group in your own industry.

CONSIDER A CLIENT-APPRECIATION EVENT

Client appreciation events are as powerful as they are overlooked. Our experience has taught us that most businesspeople fail to hold appreciation events even though the potential upswing is great.

Here's how it works.

First, partner with a friend (or two) and pick a date and venue that works for everyone. When picking the date, you'll want to allot a good eight weeks for planning. We recommend partnering with a colleague, especially if you're doing this for the first time, because doing so will help ensure success by taking some of the pressure off yourself and sharing the load. No one wants to go to an event and find only five people there! If you partner with two people, even if each person only has five folks show up, you still have 15 people attending, and you're in good shape. Also, partnering is a good way to share the cost and responsibilities to avoid feeling overwhelmed with event-planning responsibilities.

Second, you'll want to set up an agenda. We prefer two-hour events that include appetizers that the hosts provide plus a cash bar if appropriate. A good time to have this would be from 4 to 6 P.M. so you catch people who are leaving work and looking for a social event. We also like this time because it doesn't take away from "work time" where people might be less inclined to want to attend.

In terms of cost, and depending on how many people attend, you're looking at $200 to $300 each, which most business professionals consider manageable.

Your last step is to pick up the phone and start making calls. Call past clients, current clients, referral partners, and pretty much anyone who you think could benefit your business. This is the fun part!

All you have to say is, "Hey, just wanted to let you know that we're having a client appreciation event coming up in a few weeks. Free appetizers and a cash bar, and I wanted to know if you'd like to come." There's no need to overcomplicate this part; it's very easy. To keep track of the number of people attending, you can set up an Eventbrite (www.eventbrite.com) registration page.

As far as the event itself, again, keep it simple. During the two hours, you'll want to mix and mingle, and depending on how you feel, have someone take pictures. Afterward, you can post the photos on your website and potentially have people share them on social media.

About 45 minutes into the event, you and your partner(s) can address everyone there in a quick talk during which time you thank everyone for attending. You also have the option to let people know about the specific referral you're looking for (e.g., more speaking engagements, more realtor contacts), that way they can be on the lookout.

And that's it.

From there, you can get a drink and have fun talking with people. Afterward, you can individually follow up with people who said they might have some potential referrals for you.

The real magic actually has nothing to do with the event itself, but rather the dialogue before, during, and after. In other words, just by picking up the phone and making calls to invite folks, you'll find yourself running into people who were "just thinking about you" and are "glad you called." Seriously. It happens all the time. The same thing happens when you're talking to folks at the event.

For this reason, you can even let people invite a friend or two. If you go with the idea that "birds of a feather flock together," then having your guests bring a guest is an efficient way to get to know likeminded people.

MAKE CALLS TO PAST CLIENTS

Even if you don't hold a client appreciation event, you can still call past clients to see how they are doing. We know this suggestion is an easy one to neglect doing because of how busy we all get with our day-to-day work, but making calls to people you've done work with is a great way to generate business and get more referrals. If you haven't done this before, you'll want to go back 12 months and write down the names of everyone with whom you've worked. From there, call everyone on your list to check in and see how they're doing.

In a perfect world, we recommend coinciding this call with an upcoming holiday; New Year's Eve, Thanksgiving, Memorial Day, Independence Day, and Labor Day all work great for clients in the U.S.

Why?

Because it's a great conversation starter to say something along the lines of:

"Hey, John, long time no talk! How are you?"

"Fine, thanks, how are you?"

"Great! I know it's been awhile since we've chatted, but with Labor Day coming up, I figured I'd just reach out to some folks and see what they've been up to. I know last time we talked you were doing X. What's the update on that so far?"

And off you go.

Again, if you make an hour's worth of calls to past clients, we can just about guarantee that someone will say, "I'm so glad you called! I was literally just thinking about you last week. Do you have a second to talk?" Give it a try and see what happens.

INCLUDE A P.S. IN YOUR EMAIL SIGNATURE

Making a brief addition—a P.S. message—to your email signature is easy but is not used very often. At the end of your automated signature, include something like this:

P.S. A great referral for me would be someone who brings in speakers for their organization, so if you know someone who needs a speaker in the areas of Marketing, Mindset, and Personal Achievement, I'd appreciate it if you mention my name. Thanks!

A message very similar to that goes out on all of Brian's emails. You'd be surprised the amount of referrals those simple words generate.

If you really want to kick it up a notch, then consider changing your message every two or three months. This can be especially useful for people who work in industries that are seasonal. In March, you're asking for one type of referral, and then in June, you're mentioning a different one. This helps keep your message fresh and gets people to pay attention to your email signature!

THE BOTTOM LINE

Referrals do not happen overnight. They are the product of time, thought, and a good bit of energy put toward deepening the relationships of those around you. But when you get organized, and really structure your referral-generating activities into a formalized strategy like we outlined above, we feel you will absolutely find an increase in referral-based business. Good luck!

26

Keeping Your Social Capital Balance Sheet in the Black

Referrals are the lifeblood of just about everyone's business, and we want to share what we consider to be the missing ingredient in generating more referrals.

Insufficient social capital.

If you recall, social capital is the currency of networking. It's what prompts people to freely suggest your name when they hear of an opportunity—or not. Your social capital is an indicator of how well you know a person and how well they know you. It is a key ingredient for building a thriving referral business.

Allow us to explain. Think of your relationships with others like various bank accounts, where you might have high balances with some people but not so high with others. And similar to financial capital (e.g., money), the amount of social capital you have with others in your network will have a very real impact on how successful you are in generating referrals.

If people know, like, and trust you to a high degree (high social capital), then they will be much more likely to refer your business than if not.

This is why we believe social capital is a key missing ingredient with many less-than-successful people. Those folks tend to have only a surface-level relationship with others in their network. In other words, they know just enough about their referral sources' businesses to get by, but they don't actually know a lot about the people themselves (and vice versa). But you need a deep relationship with quite a few people to run a successful referral-based business—often two to three

IVAN

Alex was what I would call a casual business associate, but from early on after our introduction, every time I spoke to him, he invested in the relationship. He gave me ideas, gave me his time, he even did some work on a website for me. He invested . . . and invested . . . and invested.

I kept asking him how I could help him—to return the favor and reciprocate for all the kindnesses and great help he'd been to me. His answer every time was, "I don't need anything. I'm happy to do this."

This went on for almost a year. Every two to three months, Alex would show up on my radar and do something for me.

Then, one time, he phoned me and said, "I have a favor to ask ..." and I stopped him right there before he could say anything else.

"Yes!" I said.

"But you didn't even hear what the favor is!" laughed Alex.

I replied that I didn't have to hear what the favor was. I told him I knew him well enough to know he was not going to ask me something impossible and that he had invested so much into our relationship that I would do anything in my power to help him.

When he told me what he needed, it was easy—a small promotion by me for one of his services. It was such a big thing for Alex and something easy for me. I was happy to do it!

In my career, a huge number of folks have come to me and asked me to promote something for them. The thing is, the majority of those who contact me have never actually met me or had a previous conversation with me. They've never invested in the relationship, yet they want a withdrawal from it!

Before you ask for a withdrawal, make sure to make an investment and build a deep referral relationship.

dozen referral partners, although that can vary according to your business.

Could you take $100 out of a bank account that only has 50 bucks in it?

Of course not!

Yet that's what people do every day when they ask for a referral (making a "withdrawal") with a person where they don't have the necessary social capital to make that request.

BUILD SOCIAL CAPITAL FROM WITHIN

So what are some things to consider when building up your social capital with others in your network?

Well, check out these questions below, and if you can answer yes to most or all of the following points about a person and her business, you would have a pretty deep referral relationship:

- You trust them to do a great job and take great care of your referred prospects.
- You have known each other for at least one year.
- You understand at least three major products or services within their business and feel comfortable explaining them to others.
- You know the names of their family members and have met them personally.
- You have both asked each other how you can help grow your respective businesses.
- You know at least five of their goals for the year, including personal and business goals.
- You could call them at 9 o'clock at night if you really needed something.
- You would not feel awkward asking them for help with either a personal or business challenge.
- You enjoy the time you spend together.
- You see each other on a regular basis—in both business and personal situations.
- You enjoy seeing them achieve further success.
- They are "top of mind" regularly.

● You have open, honest talks about how you can help each other further.

You may be shocked at the level of personal knowledge required for a deep referral relationship, and you may want to argue that referrals should be all about business.

We completely disagree.

Referrals are personal.

When you give a referral, you give a little of your reputation away. You need to know the person that is going to affect your reputation. It takes a lot to develop this type of relationship, but those who do will certainly succeed at building a business from referrals.

27

Symptoms of a Referral

One of the tricky things about generating more "word-of-mouth" business is the feeling that you aren't doing anything that directly ties to getting more referrals. In other words, you go to networking events, but you're told to build "relationships" first and wait for the business to come.

You're then told to join a referral group, but provide referrals to others first, and then the business will come.

Maybe you even try public speaking or publishing an online newsletter, but even there, you're told to provide excellent value first . . . and then the business will come!

And while in a relationship economy, all three of those strategies are 100 percent true (you have to build visibility and credibility before profitability can come into being), they can sometimes feel like passive steps to take for an action-oriented business professional.

So we've got some good news for you. Here's a technique you can start using immediately that will directly lead to you generating more word-of-mouth business.

Educate people on the "symptoms" of a good referral so when they're out in the field, they'll immediately know what to look for in a potential ideal client.

If you went to the doctor's office and told him that you had a sore throat, a headache, and were sneezing all the time, he'd probably ask you if you've been outside a lot. Depending on your answer, he might prescribe an anti-allergen medicine, since based on your symptoms, it sounds like you're suffering from hay fever or something along those lines.

Now notice what happened.

You didn't walk into the doctor's office saying that you thought you had hay fever and asking if he could please provide some relief. No, you gave him the symptoms first, and then he translated that into a prescription.

What if the same thing could happen in your business?

What if you coached your referral partners on how to spot the "symptoms" associated with people looking to use your service, as opposed to just saying, "If you run into someone looking for a [fill in your industry] that would be a great referral."

TOP-OF-MIND PROBLEMS

One way to do this is by identifying what Callan Rush, speaker, coach, and author of Wealth thru Workshops, refers to as the "top-of-mind" problems of your prospective clients. She advocates identifying those first, then inserting them into all of your marketing materials.

To get you thinking on this, you might want to ask yourself: "What do you suspect is the greatest challenge that your clients face on a regular basis?"

Obviously, they will be different depending on your market and the types of businesses/consumers you're talking to, but for the sake of discussion, let's say you're a coach and entrepreneurs are a market you're looking to target.

What is a top of mind problem for them?

How about getting more business?

For most entrepreneurs, they want to get more clients but oftentimes don't have a big advertising or marketing budget to get the word out.

"No problem," they think. "Let me do some networking and get clients through word of mouth."

Except now they face a different problem: feeling like they are networking and meeting a ton of new people but not getting any bottom-line business!

And as a coach, that's a perfect referral for Brian because his business offers extensive resources to help with that very issue.

To facilitate referrals, Brian educates his referral partners on that specific "symptom" or condition. He uses language similar to this: "If you run across someone who feels like they're networking all of the time, but for whatever reason hasn't gotten as much business as they'd like, could you refer them to me?" Notice how this is very different from, "If you see someone out networking, send them my way." The first example talks about the problem, while the second just looks at the action or what they're doing.

If you're unsure of what your clients' top-of-mind problems might be, don't despair. Another approach involves looking at "trigger points" that might be associated with a potential transaction in your field. A trigger point is an event or scenario that triggers a person to have a new need.

Realtors, for example, can use the trigger point approach. Instead of just saying, "If you run into someone looking to buy or sell a home, point them in my direction," a realtor can be more specific with the circumstances surrounding the target market before a future home buyer needs an agent. These circumstances are the trigger points.

As an example, if first-time home buyers are one of your target markets, you can educate your referral partners on some potential triggers leading up to the transaction of a home. These triggers might include:

- People who are recently engaged or getting married and going about the task of planning their lives together (of which buying a house is certainly one step).
- Couples who just had a baby and might be looking to "move up" in their living arrangements.
- Couples whose kids have just left the nest for college and are now looking to downsize.

Those are all symptoms of a good referral because they relate to activities that usually result in buying or selling a home.

THE TRIGGER POINT APPROACH

The following three steps will help you generate more word-of-mouth business by using the trigger point approach.

Step #1: Identify your ideal client. In a perfect world, what does that person look like, and where is he trying to go?

Step #2: Identify either some common "top-of-mind" problems that person may have or some "triggers" commonly associated with him hiring your services.

Step #3: Set up networking meetings with each individual referral partner to educate them on those symptoms.

Once you do this, you'll be well on your way to increased networking and word of mouth success!

28

Gaining Their Confidence

When it comes to getting referrals from your network, confidence is a vital component—not your confidence, but the confidence your fellow network members have in you. None of them wants to risk their personal reputation by referring business, information, or contacts to a stranger. Even though you may have known many of your fellow networkers for quite some time, until they've gained a certain level of confidence that referring contacts to you will not harm their reputation with their clients, associates, friends, or family, you're still a stranger.

What exactly is this level of confidence? The time-confidence curve shown in Figure 28.1 illustrates the dynamics of the process. Your success in getting referrals depends partly on your competence, of course, but more on how far up the confidence curve the referrer's confidence in you has progressed. If you're at point B in the relationship, you've known each other for a while, but you still haven't quite achieved the necessary confidence level with this person to get a referral from her. When you reach point C, she'll feel comfortable recommending you to friends.

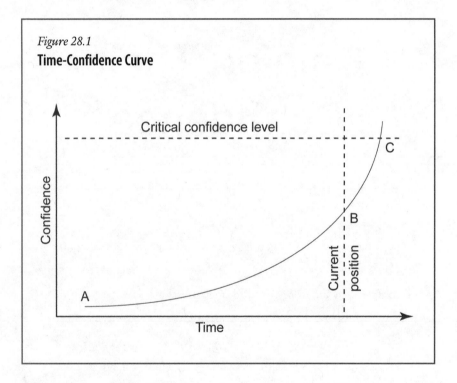

Figure 28.1
Time-Confidence Curve

GETTING THERE

How long will it take you to reach the critical level of confidence with your networking friends? Aside from the quality of your products or services, this depends on four main factors.

1. Your Profession

The more significant the business being referred, the greater the risk to the referrer's reputation. If you're a florist, it may take only a week or two for people who try your services to recommend you on the basis of their experience with you. The risk associated with referring a florist is usually small, unless you're bidding on a large corporate account that also may be your referrer's top client. If you're a lawyer, accountant, or investment advisor, it may take you six months or a year to reach the critical confidence level. However, since the stakes are higher, your referrer stands to gain more if the results are successful (see Figure 28.2). She will enhance her reputation as someone who knows the right people to get things done.

No matter what line of work you're in, if you don't perform well, your referrer will learn of it, and your progress on the confidence

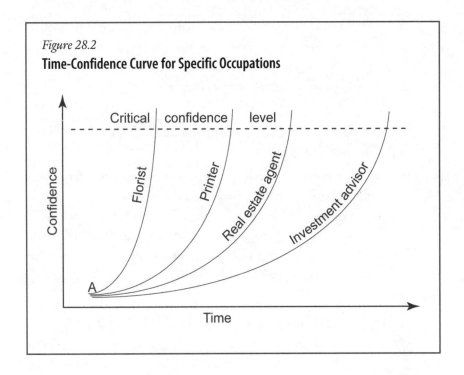

Figure 28.2
Time-Confidence Curve for Specific Occupations

curve will drop back to zero. You may not get another referral from that source, but if you do, it will take longer the second time. Third time? Don't ask.

2. How Well You Educate Others About Your Business

Don't assume that your fellow networkers understand your company or industry well enough to refer you confidently. Most have enough of a job keeping up with their own business and personal concerns. You have to educate them and keep on educating them as long as you're in business. The best way is to speak to large, receptive groups; a networking group is ideal, because everybody is expected to address the group at regular intervals. Make your presentation interesting and stimulating. Tell them how your product or service improves business or life. Tell them who, what, when, where, and how. Each time you speak, present a new aspect of your business. Let your knowledge and eloquence persuade them that you are very good at what you do. They will grow confident that you cannot seriously injure their reputations with their contacts, and your name will come to mind whenever a referral opportunity arises.

3. The Help You Give Others in Moving up Their Own Referral Confidence Curves

If you can endorse the quality of products or services offered by a networking partner—that is, increase others' confidence in him— your partner will be disposed to return the favor. Testimonials from one or two of your partners may, in turn, trigger a much larger and more valuable referral from another partner who was waiting for more evidence before taking a risk on you.

4. The Time You Invest in Learning About Others' Businesses

If you want someone to learn about the value of your products or services, you have to spend time learning about the value of his. The best way to do this is one-on-one: "John, I'd like to be able to refer more business to you, but I need a deeper understanding of what your company does and how you operate. Could we get together one day next week to discuss this?" Although you don't say so, John understands that he will learn something more about your business at the same time. Serious master networkers meet regularly to raise each other's understanding of their businesses.

STAYING FOR THE LONG HAUL

It's not always easy to know how far you've progressed up your confidence curve. Many networkers spend a lot of time and effort trying to build others' confidence in them, then on the brink of success, grow discouraged and stop attending meetings. How would you feel if someone found you a terrific referral about two weeks after you dropped out of sight?

Here's what you can do to gain perspective on your efforts and the results they are producing. Ask yourself the following four questions, and keep asking them over and over until you have attained success and the answers become obvious.

1. Am I being realistic about the time it will take, in my profession, to gain the critical level of confidence?
2. Am I regularly making stimulating, educational presentations to my fellow networkers about the value I provide to my clients?
3. Am I doing business with others in my group so I can give them dynamic testimonials and steer business to them in hopes they will return the favor?
4. Am I meeting regularly with my networking colleagues to learn about their businesses so I can confidently refer my contacts to them?

If you're following these simple tactics, then you are well along the road to getting all the referrals from others' networks that you deserve.

This material was adapted from an article by Martin Lawson in *Masters of Networking: Building Relationships for Your Pocketbook and Soul*, by Ivan Misner and Don Morgan (Bard Press, 2000).

Leveraging New Contacts

We go to networking events to meet new people and generate interest in our firm. Meeting people is an essential part of the networking process. If you're just getting started, it's where you'll spend most of your networking time, but even in a mature network, you'll devote some of your time to adding new contacts to your network—people who can help your business, put you in touch with other people they know, or simply provide you with valuable information.

But for a true networker, meeting people is only the first step in a long, continuing process.

Ultimately, your objective as a networker is to have a broad network of contacts that you can call on to help you solve problems and rustle up new business. If you intend to achieve that objective consistently, reliably, and profitably for as long as your business lasts, many of your relationships will have to be deep, trusting, and mutually beneficial associations.

At the event itself, it's tough to have a conversation that lasts longer than a couple of minutes. That's why you should never expect to do much business at a networking event, especially with people you've just met. Nevertheless, you don't have to wait until your relationships are mature in order to begin discovering business opportunities for your new contacts and yourself. In fact, it's often a good way to kick-start a new relationship.

The secret is in the follow-up.

GETTING TO THE NEXT STAGE

How can you move a relationship with someone you just met to the point where she feels comfortable passing you a referral? It depends in part on how you came into contact with her in the first place. Let's say you did so while giving a brief presentation to a group of people who are in your target market. Assuming you did a good job, then you absolutely have the possibility of receiving a referral, even though you just met. Why? Because the presentation moved you from visibility to credibility in her mind (Chapter 10: Building Quality Relationships Through the VCP Process), and now she's probably willing to risk her reputation and recommend you to someone she knows.

The same thing is true when you're out networking. If you have a good conversation with someone and truly add value to the conversation, then moving from visibility to credibility isn't that difficult, and you'll be in great shape for getting some referral-based business. What's more, it's not terribly important whether the person is someone you might do business with directly. Even if your businesses don't match up, the other person might have information that's useful or might know other people you'd like to get in contact with. It's often worthwhile developing a networking relationship with people who have little in common with you because they can bring an entirely new network into contact with yours and broaden your business horizons.

Just bear in mind that even if there is a strong possibility that you're going to do business with this new contact, it's probably not going to happen there at the networking event, where conversations last anywhere from an eye-blink three minutes to a long-winded seven. Instant business is not likely to be had, but if you follow up with a quick note a few days later, you can make some one-to-one time and come up with ways the two of you can help each other. That meeting is where you'll have your best opportunity for a quick referral.

Here are steps to leverage your new contacts.

Step #1: Segment Your Contacts into Three Groups

The first order of business, after you've met a lot of new people and come home with a pocketful of business cards, is to perform a little triage. You need to separate the people you think might become new clients or referral partners right now from the ones who might be valuable contacts sometime in the future but not right away. Let's call the first group (potential direct business) your A list, the second group (potential referral partners) your B list, and the third group (people you didn't connect with for whatever reason) your C list. When you enter them into your customer relationship manager (more on that in Chapter 10: Building Quality Relationships Through the VCP Process), this would be one good criterion to include (along with type of business, address, phone number, event where you met, and others).

BRIAN

One of the biggest mistakes people make when networking is thinking it's just about running around the room collecting as many business cards as possible. I've tried telling them that's not networking—it's face-to-face cold calling—but I find myself running into some holdouts from time to time. No problem.

Here's what you can do.

I have a dog whose name is Barley. He's a 55-pound Shiba Elnu, which means he doesn't like cats and he looks like a fox. Barley is a very well-trained, well-behaved dog. If you'd like to "network" and collect business cards at an event, here's what you can do. You can hire Barley ($15/hour, two hour minimum + travel) to attend your next event. We'll put a satchel around him (like a horse), where on one side we'll place a stack of your business cards, along with a sign that says "Take one" and on the other side we'll have a pocket that says, "Leave your card here."

We'll then drive Barley up to the event, send him into the room, and return two hours later to collect Barley and his new stack of business cards. (I'm confident he'll come out with a big stack because he's very well trained and people really do love him.)

Now after you take those cards from his side pocket (and make sure to walk him, since he'll probably need to use the restroom after all of that hard work), my question to you is very simple: did Barley just network?

What? Of course not. He's a dog. How could he possibly have networked . . . by getting a stack of business cards?

Again, it sounds ridiculous, but that's how more than a few business professionals approach their networking. As a game of who can get the most cards—and it doesn't make any sense. (But if you're still on the fence and would like to contact me about potentially contracting Barley's services, please feel free.)

Step #2: For the A's and B's, Initiate a Three-Step Follow-Up Formula

Since "follow up" is a challenge for a lot of people (and with good reason), we recommend a simple system that even the busiest of business professionals can implement right away. It's called the "24/7/30 System."

When you meet someone at a networking event, drop them a note within the first 24 hours. It can be a personal handwritten note or an email.

Handwritten notes are traditional, but they're going the way of the dinosaur in today's texting, emailing, instant everything world, which of course means that writing your invitation on paper will make you stand out from the crowd. On the other hand, who has time to buy a card, find a stamp, look up the address, fill the inkwell, pluck an ostrich plume, and scratch out the message? If you are trying to decide what method you want to choose—handwritten note or an email—we recommend you choose whatever approach you will do consistently.

In the body of your note, let the recipient know you enjoyed meeting her. Then, either mention that you hope your paths will

IVAN

All things being equal, a handwritten note is traditionally considered the best way to follow up. The problem is that I just don't do it consistently. Is it really the best method if you know you're not going to do it reliably? I don't think so. That's why I prefer to follow up with an email message, a phone call, or, better yet, a card (using something like the SendOutCards system, at www.SendOutCards.com, an easy, convenient online service). Those are the things I'm in the habit of doing, and I'm most likely to follow up in a timely way if I stick to what I do best.

cross again or invite her to a coffee connection where you can talk about different ways to help each other. Which option you use depends on how deep you feel the connection was, along with her ability to refer potential business your way. Your likelihood of inviting her to coffee will typically correlate with her potential to become a valuable referral partner.

Whether you follow up via email or with a handwritten note, keep it simple and make this process consistent.

Within seven days, connect on social media with all of the people you put into the A and B categories. Make a connection via LinkedIn or Facebook. Follow them on Twitter or join them on Google+. Find ways to connect and engage via the social media platforms you and they use the most. Do not do this as a way to sell to them; do it as a way to start establishing a meaningful connection with them.

Within 30 days, reach out to them to set up a face-to-face meeting. If you live near each other, meet in person. If you are far away from one another, set up a meeting via Skype or by phone. At these meetings, find out more about what they do, and look for ways to help them in some way. Don't make it a sales call; make it a relationship-building opportunity. Keep reading for more information about how to navigate these first one-to-one meetings.

If you use the 24/7/30 System to follow up with people you meet, you will establish a powerful routine that will help you to make your networking efforts meaningful and successful. Use technology to help remind you to follow up at the appropriate intervals. After you send the first note or email, set up reminders on your phone or calendar to follow up at one week and one month out. Remember, you want these folks to know you enjoyed meeting them, and you want to keep the door open for doing business with them later on if a good opportunity arises—this is why the late, great motivational speaker and author Jim Rohn used to say, "The fortune is in the follow-up."

IVAN

It's important to connect and engage with your network via the social media platforms they use more than the ones you use. I learned this lesson in a very unusual way.

A few years ago, my children all moved out and were on their own. It soon struck me that I was communicating regularly with them using completely different methods. My eldest would not respond to emails—ever. She wouldn't even answer the phone when I called her. I discovered, however, that when I texted her, she responded immediately. I even tested this once by calling her... no answer. Then, I texted her... immediate response. So, rather than try to get her to move over to my preferred platform, I figured that in order to keep a good line of communication open with her, I would mostly text her. It was great. We started talking more (albeit by text).

My second daughter wouldn't use email, didn't use the phone (to talk), and wouldn't consider texting (it was so old school). No, she communicated by the app WhatsApp! (www.whatsapp.com). Now, I had no idea how to use WhatsApp (I barely know how now). However, my wife pointed out that if I wanted to keep a line of communication open with her, I needed to download WhatsApp. I did. I still have no idea how to use it other than send a text to my daughter whereby she almost immediately responds.

My son didn't use email, didn't use the phone (to talk), wouldn't consider texting, and didn't use WhatsApp! What was I to do? Then, I realized that he is a big online gamer and he was using a platform called Steam (available on the app store). I also discovered that Steam Mobile had an instant messaging feature. So, I downloaded Steam and purchased a game so that I could instant message him. Yes, that's right; I bought a game so I could talk to my son. As crazy as it sounds, it worked. If I called, emailed, messaged him on any social media platform, I'd get no response. None. However, if I saw him online and messaged him, I'd get an instantaneous response! Success.

The bottom line is that if I wanted to communicate with my children, I needed to use their platforms, not mine. This taught me a lesson in networking. If I want to stay connected to the people I meet through my networking efforts, I need to go where they are, not stay where I am. It is another lesson in networking that it's not about me, it's about them.

This applies to face-to-face networking opportunities as well as online opportunities. If building a powerful network is important to you, go where your connections are and don't expect them to always come to you.

If you'd like to dig deeper into this material, please see *Avoiding the Networking Disconnect: The Three R's to Reconnect* by Ivan Misner and Brennan Scanlon (En Passant Publishing, 2015).

Step #3: Getting to Know Your New Contact over Coffee

What do you do when you meet your new contact at the coffeehouse? Get there first and pick out a good table. When he arrives, smile, shake hands, and make sure he's seated in a good spot, not in the glare of that car windshield. Chat a bit about small stuff (weather, traffic) to get the conversation started. After a couple of minutes of this, suggest going to the counter to order. As you're standing in line, you can chat about your coffee preferences or perhaps what you'd recommend.

After coming back to the table, here's what you say: "Now, I remember in our last conversation you said you were a [occupation]. I know we talked a little about it before, but maybe you could fill in the blanks and tell me more about what you do."

That is an absolute can't-miss, knock-it-out-of-the-park opening, guaranteed to get him talking about himself and his business. So far, so good. After he's done with answering the initial volley, here are some good follow-up questions:

- So, how long have you been doing this?
- How did you get into this line of work?
- Where are your favorite places to network?
- How do you go about getting new business?

That last one might seem a little odd, but it's absolutely vital to the meeting. It gets him thinking about the ways new customers come to know about him, including referrals. So, later on in the discussion when you ask for business, either with him or with someone he knows, it won't seem like you're coming out of left field. At this point, your contact will probably say that most of his business comes from word-of-mouth.

"Interesting," you say. "Tell me a little bit about your typical client. Do you work mostly with consumers, businesses . . . ?" You're trying to get a feel for his client profile. What does his typical client look like? Does he work primarily with businesses or consumers? Small companies or large? Locally or nationally?

Fork in the Road

Fifteen or 20 minutes into the conversation, you should have a pretty good picture of his ideal client. You now have three choices:

Option 1. If you know someone who can use his services directly, you say, "Well, you know, I have a friend who can really use your services. Would it be okay if I gave her a call and the two of you exchanged information? I think she'd get a lot out of meeting you."

Option 2. If you don't know someone who can use his services directly, don't panic. This happens more often than not, but you can still help him out. Let's say your new contact targets small- to midsize-technology companies. You might not know of a director who fits that prospect profile, but perhaps you do know of someone who's involved in the National Association of Technology Directors. (There's an association for everything.) You could give your new contact this person's name and offer to try to arrange a meeting or maybe even an opportunity to give a presentation at one of the group's conferences. Even though you might not know of someone directly who could use your contact's services, you might know of someone who could clearly move this person's business forward.

Option 3. If you don't know anyone at all who can help, that's fine, too. Just say, "You know, Jim, I can't think of anyone off the top of my head who could use your services, but if I do, is it all right for me to get back to you?" As long as you show you're genuinely interested in helping him out, your new contact should be pleased with that.

Step #4: Asking for a Referral (Finally!)

Yes, we know. You thought we'd never get to this part!

But here's the deal: if we did this right away (ask for a referral), before you had a chance to get to know the person, and establish a rapport, well . . . let's just say that the results would be far less appealing.

Why?

Because our society has become so skeptical and distrustful that most people are looking out only for themselves. Even though this person agreed to meet with you for coffee, he still is not totally onboard.

However, you invested in the relationship by:

a) Creating a visible identity at the event
b) Following up via email or with a handwritten note inviting him out to coffee
c) Spending the first 30 minutes figuring out how you can help him

After doing all three of those things, you've earned the right to ask for help. The best part is that the person will likely ask how he can help.

That's right.

He will ask you.

You just spent a good bit of time helping him, so it is natural he will respond in kind by asking how he can help you, too.

When he asks, that is your opportunity to share your USP, which we talked about in Chapter 23: Telling Your Company's Story, and to take your time while saying it. Then to continue the dialogue start providing some examples of what a good referral is for you.

You can refer to Chapter 27: Symptoms of a Referral, where we talk about "symptoms of a referral." The point is to give this person a good feel as to how he can help. Obviously you'll want to answer any questions he might have, but other than that, you should be in good shape.

In other words, at the end of this process you should have a referral in hand of someone who can do business with you (or is a terrific connector to your target market) or depending on your service, this person might even sign up themselves! (But remember; don't count on that because you're there to build a relationship—not to sell.)

Regardless, you should be well on your way toward generating business as a result of your coffee connection.

30

The Power of Your Database

A s you build relationships with your contacts, you'll likely find that it is difficult to keep a schedule for communicating with your network without the assistance of a Customer Relationship Manager, or CRM. (You might have heard the term CMS, which stands for Contact Management System, and for the sake of our discussion is the same thing.) It is our belief—and backed by some trusty statistics—that a CRM is a critical tool to move your business forward.

According to www.Salesforce.com, a popular CRM system, the average companies using Salesforce see:

- 27 percent increase in sales revenues
- 32 percent increase in lead conversion
- 34 percent increase in customer satisfaction
- 56 percent faster deployment

With results like that, we think it's shortsighted when people think they don't need one.

A CRM does not have to be complicated. To organize and set up your system, we encourage you to enter each person's first name, last name, phone number, and email address. Those are our non-negotiable categories.

You can also add the following optional categories by which you can filter information.

- Your relationship (if the person is a customer, client, referral partner, etc.)
- City/state (if you travel and meet people outside your immediate community)
- VCP status (where the person is along the VCP Process)

The VCP status category can be particularly useful. (VCP refers to the visibility, credibility, and profitability we talked about in Chapter 10: Building Quality Relationships Through the VCP Process.) When you include this type of data in your database, you'll be able to see where to focus your follow-up efforts.

Let's use a networking event as an example. You attended the event and met ten folks, and out of those people, you made a connection with five. You emailed the five, from which three responded. Subsequently, you had a coffee connection with each, and two of those three people passed you a referral. Those two people would certainly be connections with whom you want to remember and to stay in touch. With a VCP component in your CRM, you can do exactly that.

The initial five people you followed up with would go under "V" in your CRM when you first entered them in the database after the event and emailed them. (We don't recommend including in your database the other five people you met but didn't follow up with because if you didn't connect or follow up, then you're just cluttering your database.) Now, assume that all three face-to-face meetings went well—you impressed each person with your knowledge, wit, and intellect.

After the meetings, you should update your database by moving those three people each to a "C" because they view you as a credible resource. Of those three, the two who gave you a referral get upgraded to the "P" label in your database.

Why is taking these extra steps so important?

This process gives you another tool in your toolkit, so to speak, to generate more referrals. Experience has taught us that you'll want to stay in touch with two groups of people: the P's and C's. The P's already gave you a referral, so they are likely to again. The C's view you as a credible resource and are just one step away from sending you some business.

Assume you have been diligently adding people to your database as you meet them, and then updating their status along the VCP Process as appropriate. Also assume summer has come, and business has slowed. You have extra time on your hands to reconnect with people. Your ability to do it in a targeted, effective manner is limited only by a simple search you can do in your database in a matter of a minute.

You are becoming a networking pro. Most people are unable to reconnect with quality connections because they never implemented a formalized referral strategy (see Chapter 25: Getting More Referrals with a Formalized Referral Strategy) and they don't remember who helped them in the past. They literally don't remember.

A CRM solves that problem. You can quickly search the VCP category and email everyone who assisted you in the past.

Another field we like is the relationship field—where you list whether the person was a customer or a client of yours. Brian uses this list to contact past clients and see how things are going. During that time, he continues to present himself as a resource for potential future work.

CHOOSING A CRM

We realize that choosing a CRM can be an overwhelming process. Here are some options.

Less Annoying CRM (www.lessannoyingcrm.com)

Bracken King co-founded Less Annoying CRM with the intent of making a CRM that small-business clients actually like. According to their website, "business software can be annoying" because they are designed for huge companies. This results in small-business owners "paying for a million features that you don't want." We find their USP compelling: Less Annoying CRM "was designed from the ground up specifically for small businesses, so it's affordable, easy to understand, and, well, less annoying."

Vipor Plus (www.viporbit.com)

Mike Muhney, the co-inventor of ACT software has developed a new platform called Vipor Plus, from a company he co-founded called VIPorbit Software. Vipor Plus focuses on people's network management needs whether they are in a sales role or not. It goes further in that it accommodates in a single solution the ability to maintain not only contacts in users' business networks but also their personal ones as well, through its Orbit categorization structure. Further, those contacts can be in unlimited Orbits, meaning both in a business and a personal database, such as a customer who is also a golfing buddy. The power comes into play with all the things you can do with the contacts that are within a particular Orbit. Each of your contacts can be stored more efficiently and productively without losing that all-important personal touch.

Contactually (www.contactually.com)

According to its website, "Contactually is always thinking about your relationships . . . even when you aren't. Contactually gives you everything you need to easily organize the most important people in your network and keep you from falling out of touch over time.

"First, Contactually creates a master, centralized contacts list for you by connecting your email and other business applications. Then, it works with you to organize your most valuable relationships into Contactually's Buckets and creates customized reminders that alert you when too much time has passed between interactions.

By responding to your reminders a few times a week, you'll soon discover new opportunities from people you already know."

● ● ●

The bottom line is that building a good database is the business equivalent to working out and getting enough rest. You never think you have the time to do it, but when done consistently, it makes everything else in your life run a whole lot smoother.

We challenge you to block a few hours in your schedule to set up and organize your database because our experience has taught us that it will go a long way toward your long-term business success.

CHAPTER

31

Becoming the Knowledgeable Expert

Most businesspeople are at their best in face-to-face meetings with prospects, when they've got notes and sales materials with them and are prepared for the individual they know they'll be meeting. But how can you differentiate yourself during a networking event, when time is short and the next person you meet will be a stranger?

Easy. Think of yourself as the knowledgeable expert—the kind of person who knows a good bit about a particular subject but isn't stingy with that information. A conversation with you about your business should be like talking to your neighbor about his lawn.

"Boy, your lawn looks great," you might say to your neighbor. "What are you using on it?"

"Well, I picked up a bag of Scott's last month, and it's really doing the trick. I used to go with the cheaper brand, but it just didn't seem to be working. Anyway, I've been using Scott's for a few weeks now, and it's got this lawn looking as good as new. And the best part is it also gets rid of fire ants."

"Really?" you ask.

"Yeah. It was $5.99 a bag down the street. Real easy to put on, too."

"Huh." (Pause.) "So, how do you keep all of those weeds back anyway?"

"Well, I ran across a product I'm really impressed with," says your neighbor, and he's off describing something else.

Notice how he provided valuable information without overwhelming you. Suppose that in the middle of the conversation, he had casually let it drop that he was in the lawn-care business? You'd probably consider his company the next time your yard needed work. Why? Because he obviously knew his stuff, and who wouldn't want to work with an expert in his field? Now, imagine yourself doing the same thing when talking to people about challenges in their business that relate to your field.

We call such people knowledgeable experts, and they're absolute pros in their field. They're the people who know a thing or two about their industry and are happy to share it. They also provide their expertise without saying (or even implying), "What's preventing you from making a decision today?" Nobody likes thinly veiled sales questions and very few prospects ever respond favorably to them.

People are always looking for specific help for specific problems. As a knowledgeable expert with years of experience in your field, you know the challenges your target audience is facing and how best to handle them. You're intimately familiar with what works and what doesn't. Most of all, you know what it takes to get stuff done.

But how do you demonstrate this to prospects while networking before you've asked for a sit-down meeting or even followed up over the phone? Easy: by staying on top of the industry news. In previous books, we've often talked about the virtues of reading and constantly educating yourself about your industry; here's where that time really pays off.

A good way to become the knowledgeable expert in the eyes of your potential prospects is to have a feel for some of the other networking events around town and how those events might relate to their business. Let's say that during a conversation at a chamber event one evening, a photographer tells you she's trying to meet people in advertising and public relations. You might mention that the local business owners' association holds networking events once a month and that, even though you haven't been there personally, you understand this is where ad people and marketing directors go to network. This is valuable information for your prospect—and it's valuable for you, too, because it makes you a knowledgeable resource and makes you stand out from the crowd.

Another way to parlay good information into your day-to-day networking is to become versed on a few statistics that are relevant to your prospects. For example, if you're a financial planner and you're talking with someone who expresses concern about her retirement plan, it might be good to know that three out of five working professionals won't have enough money to retire by the age of 65, according to Randy Brunson, Certified Financial Planner (CFP), Centurion Advisor Group. Then, you can follow up with a personal anecdote on how you helped a client overcome similar challenges toward securing his own financial peace of mind (notice the choice of words). Now, you're well on your way to becoming the knowledgeable expert in your prospect's eyes. Why? Because you're giving her good information on how she can personally overcome a situation that's affecting millions of people each day.

Another way to become a knowledgeable expert is to be familiar with your prospect's issues. What are her concerns? What are her specific challenges? As a financial planner, you might learn that your prospect doesn't understand the stock market and generally distrusts the financial information that companies publish. Like the rest of us, she's seen how millions of stockholders have been defrauded by corporate malfeasance and stock manipulation. She might have real concerns about investing. This is where you can help by providing reliable information to allay her concerns:

> That's an excellent point, Mrs. Smith, and believe it or not, according to a recent survey by the Centurion Advisory Group, financially fraudulent information was only involved in less than 1 percent of the total transactions conducted last year. Couple that with our firm's strict policy of full disclosure on all financial transactions, and you can see how we've worked hard to gain the trust of all our clients.

Stating facts this way can give your prospect the peace of mind she's looking for, since it shows an understanding for her concern along with a willingness to allay that fear with good, sound data. One simple statistic can help ratchet up your credibility with a relatively new contact, and it all starts by having an understanding of what your prospect's true concerns are.

Or suppose that you're a mortgage broker, and someone at a chamber says, "So what is it you do?"

"I specialize in helping people get into the home of their dreams, regardless of past credit history," you say.

"Really," he responds. "Regardless of history, huh? I always thought credit was everything when it came to financing a home."

"Well, sure, great credit is going to make my job a whole lot easier. But there are lots of ways to finance a home, without necessarily having the best credit in the world. Something I advise my clients to close out any unnecessary credit cards. Even if they have a zero balance, they can hurt your credit score when it comes to getting a loan. That, plus a solid payment history on the cards you do have, is usually enough to get you in the door—literally and figuratively."

"Is that so?"

"Oh, yes. As a matter of fact, I was working a file the other day where a couple were coming out of a bankruptcy, and because of that, they were having a tough time finding financing. A mutual friend of ours knew about the situation, referred me in, and within a couple of weeks we were working on a program I think will do the trick."

"Really?" (Pause.) "Let me get your card. I've got someone you might want to meet."

And there you go.

Notice how you were able to clearly demonstrate your expertise in a subtle, yet powerful manner? The conversation didn't feel like a pitch, just a comfortable exchange of good information in which you clearly showed that you know what you're doing. This, needless to say, will make that prospect feel more inclined to work with you.

One of the questions we often get in workshops is this: "Is it possible that I will give away too much good information and wind up not converting this new contact into a client?" Great question, since that obviously defeats the purpose of networking in the first place. Here's what we recommend: when networking, focus on demonstrating your ability to handle the problem, without giving your prospect everything he needs to know to solve it.

It's not that hard to become a knowledgeable expert. Just take a minute to read an article about your industry once a day, perhaps online where you can easily keep up with current developments. Familiarize yourself with it; remember a specific fact or statistic that you can work into a networking conversation. Then, you're good to go.

With buyers' skepticism at an all-time high, people are going to give your business only after you've made them comfortable with your expertise. The way to do that is to fill yourself up with as much knowledge as possible about your prospects' challenges, along with stories demonstrating how you've helped others in the past. When you're the knowledgeable expert, you're the go-to guy (or gal).

BRIAN

I usually talk about the prospect's business and some different things he could do to bring in more revenue. Since I'm a marketing coach by trade, my conversations always seem to gravitate toward helping others get more business. So after hearing some of their issues, throwing out some general ideas, and sharing a couple of personal stories demonstrating my expertise, I might wrap up with something like this:

Well, if we decided to work together, one of the things I'd recommend is to take a look at your business and identify two or three specific audiences, or target markets, that are most likely to use your services. You mentioned how you feel exhausted at the end of the day, working hard and doing a bunch of good things. But sometimes, it's hard to pinpoint exactly what you're accomplishing.

Having some specific target markets will help you get away from that so you don't have to feel like you're always running around from one networking event to the other, chasing the latest lead. You can have a crystal-clear focus on the people you want to meet and where they're most likely to be, which by itself should be a real boost for your business.

After that, I'd want to see some of your brochures and other marketing collateral. I know you mentioned that you just updated your website, and that's a great first step toward getting more business. I'm thinking maybe an electronic newsletter that gets people visiting your site would be a good idea, along with a link that gives them an opportunity to look at your brochure.

Obviously, we don't have time to get into that right now, but if you'd like, I can take your card, give you a call in a few days, and if we want to set up some time to talk more about this, that's absolutely fine.

In this way, I am able to incorporate our conversation into a workable game plan on what I'd recommend if we decided to work together. When the game plan is mentioned at the end of the conversation, after you've stated relevant statistics and demonstrated understanding of the prospect's issues, it's almost impossible not to be seen as the knowledgeable expert—and get a lot more business in the process.

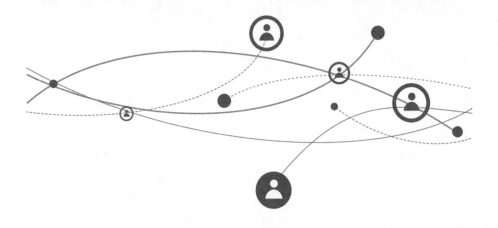

PART V

SECRETS OF THE MASTERS

32

Becoming a Referral Gatekeeper

After you've been networking for a while, you begin to see that there's a pattern to all of those connections you've been making. It's as if you're sitting in the middle of a spider web, with all the lines running outward connected to other lines, and whenever someone you're connected to makes a connection for you, you can feel the vibrations coming in from that direction. What's really happening, though, is that each person you're connected to is at the center of a web of his own.

Once you visualize how complex this web really is, you may begin to think, "What if I could be more directly connected to all those other webs out there? Would I get more referrals? Would I get a greater variety of referrals? Would I get higher-quality referrals? Is there a species of a super networker who is in direct contact with those other networkers, the ones who are connected to me only through intermediaries?"

GUARDIAN AT THE GATE

The answer is yes, there is a special type of networker who is more connected than most: the referral gatekeeper.

IVAN

When I started my first business, I knew I wanted referrals to play a key part in my overall growth strategy. The only problem was I didn't know exactly what I needed to do to accomplish that goal. So I joined some business associations, started networking more, and did everything I could to generate more word-of-mouth marketing. Though all of that worked to a large extent, it finally dawned on me how I could supercharge the whole process.

I began to realize that I wasn't the only one trying to get more sales through referrals; a lot of other business professionals were trying to do the same thing. But it also occurred to me that the people I knew were different from the people the next person knew, who were different from the next person's contacts, and so on. I might get a few referrals from my own network, but I could probably get a few more referrals from the other person's network, and the ones beyond that, almost without limit.

So I thought, "What if I became the hub?" If all the other people out there were trying to do the same thing as I was, why couldn't I position myself as a gatekeeper of sorts between other people's networks? Then, if someone was buying a new home and needed a real estate agent but didn't have one in her own network, she would come to me to see whom I knew.

How did that help my business?

First, it encouraged me to continue building and deepening my relationships with others, even if I didn't think they could help me right away. Let's face it: we are all limited on time, and our natural tendency is to build relationships with those we feel can help us the most. No problem, except for one thing: you never know who the other person knows.

Even though it might not appear that way on the surface, it's always a good idea to have a lot of contacts, and becoming a gatekeeper gave me another good reason to do just that. Bob Smith might not be a good referral partner for me, but he could be ideal for Jane Doe, another person I know.

The second reason I thought this would be good for my business was the positive effect it would have on my credibility. I wanted to be the go-to guy in the business community—the person others came to if they needed a referral for anything. This meant that I would be deepening relationships with people I might not otherwise have gotten to know. Furthermore, since we all know people do business with others they like and trust, who do you think is going to get their business when they need someone like me? You got it.

With all this in mind, I drafted the following letter:

Dear _____:

I really believe in the process of referrals, and so part of the service I provide is to be sure to refer my clients and associates to other qualified businesspeople in the community.

Attached is a list of areas in which I know very credible, ethical, and outstanding professionals. If you're looking for a profession-al in a specific area I've listed, please feel free to contact me. I will be glad to put you in touch with the people I know who provide these services.

Sincerely,

Ivan Misner

Notice that I listed only professions; I didn't list names and phone numbers. I wanted my clients to contact me so I could put the referral and the contact together. I wanted to build relationships, not to become a glorified phone directory. I wanted to become known as an effective networker, and that would happen only if I made the connections myself.

Essentially, I wanted to deepen the relationships I had with my clients so they would be more likely to keep me as their service provider of choice. In our BNI groups, we say that every relationship is in one of the three phases of the VCP Process—visibility, credibility, or profitability. Obviously, you want to move as many people as quickly as possible into the profitability phase, and that's what this letter enabled me to do. I mailed it to all my clients (and prospects) four times in the first year. I didn't get a single reply until the third time, but after that, the floodgates opened and I got responses every time I sent it out.

Over time, I cultivated a reputation as a gatekeeper by doing this. I no longer had to send out my letter several times a year. People came to see me because they heard I knew a great number of businesspeople in the community. Others would ask people on my client list, "Who do you know who does XYZ?" If my contacts didn't know anyone, they would send the questioner to me.

If you are a businessperson seeking to grow your business by word-of-mouth marketing, becoming a gatekeeper will give you an enormous advantage. It's a strategy that not only gets people to contact you for referrals, but it also opens up a dialogue with them about your business and how it can help them. This, in turn, leads to more business with existing clients and new business with prospects.

On the other side of the process, the people on my list of professions, the ones to whom I referred potential customers, were impressed and grateful. They reciprocated by sending people my way, and they began to come to me when they needed a referral. It helped, of course, that I had sent each of them a copy of my letter to tell them I would be sending business their way.

As I developed my mailing list, I would drop certain people off it with whom I didn't have any further contact. One time someone who had been dropped from my list called to tell me he missed the letters! He needed a referral and had to look up an old letter of mine he had kept on file. I actually ended up doing some business with him as a result of this incident.

This is just one technique to consider when building your business through referrals. It's a touch point that puts you in contact with your clients and prospects in a way that fosters different dynamics than when you're trying to sell to them. You have something they need: referrals and contacts. Allow this to open the door for reciprocal sharing and giving. You'll be amazed at how much more business you can do with each other as a result.

HUB OF THE WHEEL

Another way to be a referral gatekeeper is to position your business as a hub firm. This is a familiar concept to experienced business networkers and is a good way to take advantage of the nature of your business if your line of work involves routine contact with other businesses. If you're a financial planner, for instance, your work with a client might involve putting him in contact with an investment counselor, a stockbroker, an insurance agent, a tax planner, and so forth. A building contractor is another familiar example; among the firms that orbit this hub are plumbers, electricians, air conditioner installers, cement companies, roofers, and many others.

Here's another example: suppose you're a wedding planner. Your business puts you in constant contact with a number of other businesses that relate to weddings: caterers, bakers, florists, photographers, jewelers, wedding chapels, and others. You can envision your business as the hub of a wheel (see Figure 32.1 on page 231).

Depending on the size and cost of the wedding, you may be in touch with different combinations of these other businesses. An expensive wedding might have you signing contracts with businesses A, C, D, E, G, and H; a less elaborate ceremony might involve only companies B, D, and F. Even though you work with businesses that compete with each other, you become a referral partner with every one of them because you refer businesses to all of them over time.

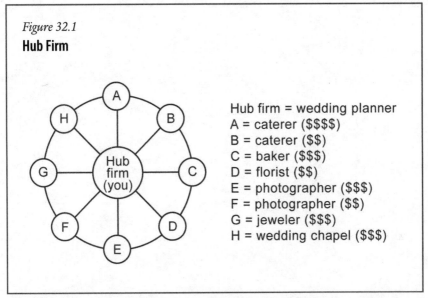

Figure 32.1
Hub Firm

Hub firm = wedding planner
A = caterer ($$$$)
B = caterer ($$)
C = baker ($$$)
D = florist ($$)
E = photographer ($$$)
F = photographer ($$)
G = jeweler ($$$)
H = wedding chapel ($$$)

Being a hub firm makes you a very powerful networker. In fact, putting yourself at the center of any network can make you a master networker in short order, able to choose the cream of the high-quality clients that will come your way.

Always Thank Your Referral Partners

Thanking your referral partners is probably one of the most underrated ways to generate more referral-based business. Why?

Because everyone loves to be acknowledged for their efforts and, in most cases, will absolutely engage in activities in which those efforts are appreciated.

But more times than not, when people get a referral, their first inclination is to blurt out "Thanks!" and then immediately focus on the person they just got referred to. While that's not necessarily a bad way of doing business, there are better ways to creatively reward your referral partners, so they not only hear your thanks . . . but feel it too.

CREATIVE REWARDS

Most people would agree that one of the best ways to consistently generate referrals is to have a system that rewards your referral partners. There are many ways you can do this, but the best way is to design creative incentives for them. However, of all the techniques for making the system work, this one seems to frustrate people the most.

The most common incentive for referrals is a finder's fee. Although a finder's fee can work in some situations, it might not be the best approach with every referral partner. Why? Because when a trusted referral partner gives you a referral, it's usually the by-product of your good relationship, and an offer of money would tend to cheapen the experience; it might even be considered an insult.

However, this doesn't mean generosity should go unrewarded. You just need to find a more creative way to say thanks.

IVAN

Years ago, I went to my chiropractor for a routine adjustment. I had referred a friend to him several weeks before who had recently been in an accident. As I walked into the waiting room, I noticed a bulletin board displayed prominently on the wall. The bulletin board read, "We would like to thank the following patients for referring someone to us last month."

There was nothing unusual about this sign; it had been there on each of my previous visits. But this time, my name was on it. I took notice and was pleased but didn't give it a second thought—until a month later, when I returned and saw that my name was no longer on it. Instantly, I thought, "Who else can I refer to the doctor so my name will be put back on the board?" For the record, I did come up with another referral for the good doctor.

Being highlighted on a bulletin board might not work for everyone, but if it worked on me, I'm sure it has a positive effect on others as well, for at least two reasons. The bulletin board is a continual reminder to patients that the office wants their referrals, and people like to be recognized for their efforts.

There are many ways to reward people for referrals, depending on the type of product or service you offer and your relationship with your referring parties. The key is to offer rewards that are attractive to as many people as possible. Some health-care professionals offer a free visit when a referral becomes a new patient. Business professionals sometimes send small gift baskets, bottles of wine, flowers, or certificates for their services or the services of other businesses in the community. Other professionals offer free estimates, samples, analyses, discounts on products or services, group discounts, or even extended warranties.

One enterprising business professional offered clients who brought him good referrals a $500 discount on their next purchase. This was a bargain. A new customer is worth many times that amount in business, and the cost of advertising, printed literature, and time spent on telephone calls, meetings, appointments, and sales calls that are typically needed to bring in a new customer can far exceed the cost of such a referral incentive. You can afford to be generous with a good referral partner, who can readily bring you more business. Incentive programs also help you sell more products or services to your existing customer base with little effort or marketing cost.

Some businesspeople use a technique known as incentive triangulation, a powerful way of leveraging other people's services to benefit your customers, clients, or patients. The concept is simple and can be designed to fit the needs or requirements of almost any business.

Here's how it works. First, you negotiate an arrangement with another local business—printer, massage therapist, jeweler, florist— to give a discount to any of your clients you send its way. Then, whenever one of your clients gives you a referral, you reward that person with your usual incentive, plus a coupon good for your prearranged discount at the other business. (See Figure 33.1.)

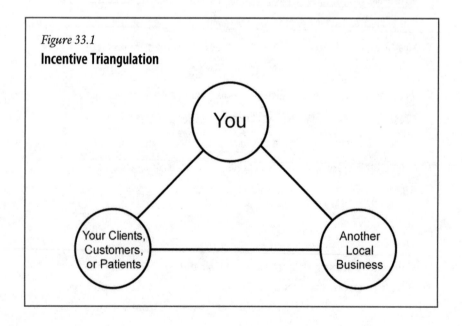

Figure 33.1
Incentive Triangulation

This form of joint venture is beneficial for all three parties. You benefit because you are providing another incentive for people to give you referrals. The other business benefits because you are recommending it to your clients. Your referrer benefits because she gets recognition for her efforts, as well as an additional product or service at a reduced rate. Granted, this type of incentive may not be appropriate for all professions, but when it works, it works well.

No matter what form of incentive program you use, the fact that you offer incentives increases your potential for generating word-of-mouth business. The question is—what type of incentive will work for you? To meet the challenge of finding the right incentive program, tap into the assistance and insights of other people. An effective way to do this is to invite about ten people you know to meet with you over lunch or dinner. Include a representative sample of your customers (or clients or patients), business associates, partners, and friends. Tell them their assignment is to think up incentives you could offer to increase your word-of-mouth-based business.

Prepare yourself well in advance. Be prepared to take copious notes or to record the meeting. Think about the topic and its ramifications; have an idea of the limits you may need to set for an incentive program, such as cost, duration, and appropriateness. Have soft drinks, note pads, a preliminary questionnaire, sample materials, a flip chart, and even a few ideas to get the ball rolling. If you're going to discuss a product, bring samples to give the group a point of reference.

Begin the session by clearly stating a specific problem. Make sure your group understands that the incentive has to be geared to the group you've targeted. Explain that you are looking for a variety of ideas and that you won't make any immediate decisions.

When your group meets, the first step is to brainstorm ideas. The concept of brainstorming was originated by Alex F. Osborn to help trigger creative ideas in advertising. Following the meal, you or a designated party can lead a brainstorming session to generate ideas on an effective incentive program for your business. For maximum creativity, everyone must fully understand and follow four basic principles. To paraphrase Osborn:

1. *Encourage freewheeling.* The wilder the ideas, the better; it's easier to tame down ideas than to think them up. Wild ideas often lead to creative solutions, but the way an idea is first presented by its originator doesn't always register with others. With a twist and turn, however, ideas seemingly from Mars are brought back to Earth and become eminently workable.

2. *The more, the better.* The greater the number of ideas people think of, the better the likelihood of a winner coming out of the selection. Don't be afraid to go to the second or third page of a flip chart. You want at least 12 ideas so you'll have plenty to work with once everyone runs out of steam.

3. *Don't rush to judgment.* Criticism of ideas must be withheld until later; otherwise you run the risk of shutting down the idea pipeline. Not only does criticism stifle creativity, but it can make the session deteriorate to a nitpicking session that goes on forever without accomplishing anything.

4. *Combine and refine.* In addition to contributing ideas of their own, participants should suggest how ideas of others could be turned into better ideas or how two or more ideas could be combined into still another idea. Some ideas that aren't workable alone become quite effective in combination.

Once you've run out of new ideas for possible incentives, review the list item by item and try to narrow it down to a manageable number. Don't worry about how you're going to do something until you've determined all the options. After most of the ideas are eliminated, spend time discussing those that are left and get feedback on which ones may be most effective. Last, select the idea or ideas you'll put into practice.

At the end of the session, if the ideas were really flying, suggest the group meet again soon. Instead of having a one- or two-time session, your group might even become an advisory board, meeting at regular intervals. Even if you meet only quarterly or semiannually, there is great value in having reconvened to discuss the challenges you're working on.

Creativity is the key to any good incentive program. People naturally like to help each other, especially when they know their efforts are successful. Let your contact know when a referral he has made comes through and be as creative as you can. There are many creative ways businesspeople reward those who send them referrals. A female consultant sends bouquets of flowers to men; a music store owner sends concert tickets; a financial planner sends change purses and money clips.

An accountant in St. Louis thanks those who successfully refer a client to him by paying for a dinner for two at an exclusive restaurant that's at least an hour's drive from their homes. This approach firmly plants the accountant in the minds of his referral sources. They won't be able to use the reward right away, because the distance requires that they plan for it. As the date approaches, because it has been planned, they'll be talking about it and probably about the accountant. Later, when the referring party runs into someone else who might need an accountant, whom do you think he'll recommend?

Another option to keep in mind is to offer different kinds of incentives for different groups of people. Are there employees, co-workers, friends, or relatives who might be able to refer your business? It always surprises us when people forget to provide incentives for the individuals working with them. You may choose to offer something completely different for your employees than you would for your clients or networking associates. Bonuses and vacation days are always a good idea, but the important thing is you need to offer something for them as well.

IVAN

Almost 20 years ago, a real estate agent I met in northern California told me that for almost six years he had offered a $100 finder's fee to anyone giving him a referral that led to a listing or sale. He said that in all that time he had given only about a dozen finder's fees, so he decided to try another kind of incentive.

Living on a large parcel of land in prime wine country, he had begun growing grapes in his own vineyard. A thought occurred to him: Why not take the next step? He began processing the grapes and bottling his own special vintage wine. After his first harvest, he had a graphic artist design a beautiful label, which he affixed to each bottle. He told all his friends that he did not sell this wine; he gave it as a gift to anyone providing him with a bona fide referral.

He gave away dozens of cases in the first three years—half the time it took him to give only one dozen cash finder's fees—yet each bottle cost him less than $10 to produce. This special vintage wine makes him infinitely more money than giving away a handful of $100 finder's fees.

About two weeks ago, I got a call from the real estate agent, who told me the following story. A woman he didn't know called him and gave him two referrals. As he wrote down the information, he asked her how she had heard of him. She said she had had dinner one night at a friend's house. She had complimented the host on his wine selection and asked him where he'd gotten it. He told her it was not found in any store and that the only way to get a bottle was to give a referral to a real estate agent he knew. She got his contact information from her friend and called him up two days later.

After giving the real estate agent the referrals, she said, "I have two referrals. Can I get two bottles?" He told me he sent her the bottles and both referrals turned into business, each costing him only $10.

Now, if you're wondering how something as simple as a bottle of wine can be such a powerful incentive for giving referrals, the explanation is really quite simple: it's special. A bottle of wine that can't be bought can be worth ten times what it costs to produce when traded for something as valuable as a business referral.

Remember, finding the right incentive is considered the biggest challenge by most individuals who want to build their word-of-mouth business. To make it easier on yourself, be sure to get opinions and feedback from others who have a significant interest in your success.

Take a few minutes to review Do You Network Like a Pro? in Appendix B of this book. This will help you prepare your own personal incentive program. Don't underestimate the value of recognizing and thanking your referral partners; they're the people who send you business.

34

Networking at Non-Networking Events

You can network anywhere, anytime, anyplace . . .even at a funeral.

For most people, that can come as a little bit of a shock, but hear us out. The key is to always **honor the event!** Networking is about building relationships. The best way to do that is to help people. It's not about going around and passing out your card, though in some situations, that's completely inappropriate. However, there are few situations that are inappropriate to find ways to help people (not sell to them) but help them in some way. That's what networking and relationship building is all about.

Most of what we've discussed so far is about networking in traditional networking venues, such as the chamber, strong-contact referral groups, and other business-oriented gatherings. If that is your framework for understanding networking, though, then you're not using its power to its fullest.

You can network anywhere, including events where it might not at first occur to you to try it—and, paradoxically, it's at these nontraditional networking settings where you'll get the most bang for your buck. Why? Because not many people think of it.

Social settings are rarely (if ever) the place to distribute marketing material, but telling people what you do in response to a question is perfectly fine. And then, depending on the situation and how it's received, a quasi-business discussion might unfold. Is this the setting to ask for business or take order? No!

Rather, you are listening to what the other person has to say and creating awareness for your business, while deepening the relationship with that person. Then, depending on how the conversation goes, you can connect via social media or even set up a follow-up phone call to "talk a little bit more about this offline, and see if there might be some ways we can help each other out."

The other benefit of networking at non-networking events is you've got the field to yourself! In other words, very few other people are doing it. This means that you have countless opportunities to develop lasting relationships with potential referral partners.

NONTRADITIONAL SETTINGS

What nontraditional settings are we referring to? Well, Christmas parties, birthday parties, Easter, Thanksgiving, Independence Day, Memorial Day, Halloween, Labor Day, and any other special occasion where people you might not normally meet get together. Even a Super Bowl party is fine—as long as you do it correctly.

But remember, the only reason this works is because networking is not just trying to sell something or passing business referrals;

it's building meaningful relationships and social capital. Master networkers understand this. That's why it's possible for them to network at non-networking events, while still honoring the event and not offending anyone.

So with that in mind, let's jump into some specifics on how to do this right.

ASK, "HOW CAN I HELP?"

Givers Gain is the number-one rule to remember. You should always be thinking, "How can I help this person?" Many of us know this and try to apply it to our relationships, but we're more inclined to do it instinctively with those in the profitability category. How can we apply it to the relationships that are in the visibility and credibility categories?

At a social event, you usually ask somebody, "How's it going?" What's the typical reply? Probably something like "Great; things couldn't be better." That's a canned response that people give because they want to be polite and because they know nobody really wants to hear their troubles. But it's not usually the whole truth.

Most people experience challenges or roadblocks that hold them back. If you adhere to the Givers Gain philosophy, you should try to make people feel comfortable sharing those issues, so then you can be a facilitator in whatever way possible. Here are some questions you can ask:

- How can I help?
- Is there anything I can do to help?
- What can I do for you?

All of these questions hit the proverbial spot when it comes to conveying your desire to assist. Then, when people respond, really listen to what they are saying so you can provide helpful input. Remember that being a good listener is one of the key characteristics of great networkers.

IVAN

Things can always be better—that is, there are surely ways you can help—but most people aren't inclined to go into detail or let others know what's going on, especially at social events. The best way to find out is to avoid generalities like "How are things?" Ask more specific questions.

In a conversation I had recently, I asked an individual how things were going and got the standard answer that things were great, the company was expanding, and business was better than expected. My next question was "Are you hitting all of your goals?" Yes, the business was exceeding all of its goals by a large margin.

Sounds like this person didn't need any help, you say? On the contrary: to me, it sounded like a big opportunity. Think about it: a company that was expanding faster than the owner had projected. What kind of help might it need?

Many consider networking just another way to get clients, but when you think in terms of building relationships, a chance to help is a big opportunity and that help can be provided in many forms, each as valuable as the next.

In this case, I was able to make some introductions that the individual was very grateful for, but it was only after getting past the generalities that I was able to figure this out.

Always plan on maximizing your networking productivity during the holiday season. Remember, networking means developing relationships, and the holidays are filled with opportunity.

BE SINCERE

If you're networking successfully at a non-networking event, people won't even know it. You're genuinely looking for ways to help other people, and your concern for the person you're talking with is plainly apparent. Anyone who is networking exclusively for personal gain comes across as shallow and insincere.

A good networker doesn't have to work at sincerity. She really cares about making connections for others, not just for herself. Some people are so accomplished and successful at networking that they are able to network virtually anywhere. No one minds you using an opportunity to share information that will benefit others, even when that exchange takes the form of a business card at a bar mitzvah.

HONOR THE EVENT

Always remember to respect the event you're attending. This one should be a no-brainer, but we all know some scorched-earth, overzealous networkers who trawl the room at a party in pursuit of a sale, any sale. They may do the same, less blatantly, at family and purely social events, but this is still the exact opposite of what networking is all about. Remember, relationships are the name of the game. Socials are a great place to get visibility and credibility, so focus on building these aspects of relationships.

35

Top Ten Ways Others Can Promote You

Has anyone ever said to you, "If there's anything I can do to help you with your business, let me know"?

And was your response, "Thank you. Now that you mention it, there are a few things I need" or did you say, "Well, thanks, I'll let you know"?

If you're like most of us, you aren't prepared to accept help at the moment it's offered. Before you can do so, you have to make the connection between specific items or services you need and the people who can supply them.

SYSTEMATIC REFERRAL MARKETING

Systematic referral marketing helps you do that by determining, as precisely as possible, the types of help you want and need. Some are simple, cheap, and quick; others are complex, costly, and time-consuming. Here are some examples of the ways others can promote you and your business.

1. *Display or distribute your literature and products.* Your sources can exhibit your marketing materials and products in their offices or homes. If these items are displayed well, such as on a counter or a bulletin board, visitors will ask questions about them or read the information. Some may take your promotional materials and display them in other places, increasing your visibility. They can include your fliers in their mailings or hand them out at meetings they attend. A dry cleaner attaches a coupon from the hair salon next door to each plastic bag he uses to cover his customers' clothing; a grocery store includes other businesses' marketing literature in or on its grocery bags or on the back of the printed receipt.

2. *Make an announcement.* When attending meetings or speaking to groups, your sources can increase your visibility by announcing an event you are involved in or a sale your business is conducting or by setting up exhibits of your products or services. They can also invite you to make an announcement yourself.

3. *Invite you to attend events.* Workshops and seminars are opportunities to increase your skills, knowledge, visibility, and contacts. Members of personal or business groups you don't belong to can invite you to their events and programs, which gives you an opportunity to meet prospective sources and clients. Even better, they could invite you to speak at their event, effectively positioning you as an expert in your field.

4. *Endorse your products and services.* By telling others what they've gained from using your products or services or by endorsing

you in presentations or informal conversations, your network sources can encourage others to use your products or services. If they sing your praises on an MP3, a DVD, or social media, so much the better.

5. *Nominate you for recognition and awards.* Business professionals and community members often are recognized for outstanding service to their profession or community. If you've donated time or materials to a worthy cause, your referral sources can nominate you for service awards. You increase your visibility both by serving and by receiving the award in a public expression of thanks. Your sources can inform others of your recognition by word of mouth or in writing. They can even create an award, such as Vendor of the Month, to honor your achievement.

6. *Make initial contact with prospects and referral sources.* Instead of just giving you the telephone number and address of an important prospect, a network member can phone, email, or meet the prospect first and tell him about you. When you make contact with the prospect, he will be expecting to hear from you and will know something about you. Better yet, your source can help you build new relationships faster through a personal introduction to that person. Ideally she would provide you with key information about the prospect while also telling the prospect a few things about you, your business, and some of the things you and the prospect have in common.

7. *Arrange a meeting on your behalf.* When one of your sources tells you about a person you should meet or someone you consider a key contact, she can help you immensely by coordinating a meeting. Ideally, she will not only call the contact and set a specific date, time, and location for the meeting but will also attend the meeting with you.

8. *Publish information for you.* Network members may be able to get information about you and your business printed in

publications they subscribe to and in which they have some input or influence. For example, a referral source who belongs to an association that publishes a newsletter might help you get an article published or persuade the editor to run a story about you. Many companies showcase topic-specific experts in their newsletters; you could become the expert in your field for some of these.

9. *Form strategic alliances with you.* Of all the kinds of support that a source can offer, this one has the greatest potential for long-term gain for both parties. When you engage in a strategic alliance, you're in essence developing a formal relationship with another business owner that says you will refer him business whenever possible and he will do the same. This works best in businesses that are complementary. For example, a handyman would find advantages in forming an alliance with a real estate agent, because they continually encounter people who need home repair work done. Conversely, a handyman probably deals with homeowners who are considering selling their homes after he's finished making repairs. Such strategic alliances can work with a number of other businesses (CPAs and financial advisors, mortgage brokers and real estate agents, hotel salespeople and event planners, and so on). The key is to find the person with the right complementary business and then make it work for both of you.

10. *Connect with you through online networks.* When people connect with you online, you can notify them about your events or projects, and you can receive the same kind of information from them. They can see your business profile and biographic data and can refer you to people in their networks. Once connected, they can provide recommendations and testimonials for the rest of your network to view.

36

Five Levels of a Referral

A referral is a referral, right? Well, not so much. Once a referral source has given you the name of a person to call, what more could you hope for?

Actually, there's quite a bit more you can expect from referrals that have been properly developed by their sources. Referrals come in several different shades. We've identified five types of referrals that vary in quality according to how much involvement your referral source has invested in preparing the referral for you. The more time and effort your source puts into qualifying, educating, and encouraging the prospect before you become involved, the higher the quality and level of that referral. Conversely, if your referral source only passes an interested prospect's name to you, most of the work of converting that prospect into a customer falls on you, and the likelihood of a successful conversion diminishes significantly.

Of course, the effectiveness of your referral network in providing you with quality referrals depends on the amount of work you do to develop your sources. There are many ways to encourage them to become active and enthusiastic members of your marketing team. The Networking Scorecard (explained in Chapter 37: The Networking Scorecard) will enable you to track the work you are doing to develop your network. By using this scorecard to keep a weekly record of your network development efforts and the quality of referrals you receive, you'll begin to see the relationship between the two. Now let's cover the five levels of referrals, ranging from nothing but a name and contact information to the "Full Monty" (which despite the movie, actually means to do everything possible). We call this the Referral Continuum, and we've ranked the levels of the continuum in order of ascending quality.

Please note that this is a "referral" continuum, not a "leads" continuum. All of these levels are true referrals not leads (including the first one). The person giving the referral knows both parties and is recommending the person providing the product or service to the person who is receiving the product or service.

Note that each level below builds upon the previous. So a Level 2 referral includes much of what is included in a Level 1 referral, and a Level 3 referral includes much of what is in Level 1 and 2 referrals, etc.

LEVEL 1: NAME AND CONTACT INFORMATION

Your referral source has recommended you to someone and shared your contact information. She has done just enough work to provide you with a phone number, address, email, or some other way of contacting the prospect *and* that prospect knows you might contact them. If the prospect is expecting your call, this is a legitimate referral—it's just not a high-level referral. That said, we'd take this over a "cold call" any day of the week!

LEVEL 2: SUPPLEMENTARY MATERIAL

In addition to the recommendation, the referral source provided either your marketing literature, website information, or other content to the prospect for their review but nothing substantially more. This additional information can positively influence the prospect by providing more material to review in addition to the referral source's verbal reference.

LEVEL 3: SHARE TESTIMONIAL

In addition to some or all of the items above, the referral source gave a personal written testimonial or a *strong* verbal recommendation about you to the prospect. He spent time talking to the prospect about his experience working with you or his understanding of other people's experience working with you. This is the first level of referral that truly involves a modicum of effort on the part of your referral source. It usually includes background information and a description of your product or service as filtered through the lens of the referral source.

Adding the element of promotion increases the effectiveness of your referral source's effort on your behalf. Promotion is advocacy—an outright recommendation of your product or service with a description of its features and benefits.

LEVEL 4: INTRODUCTORY CALL AND/OR ARRANGE A MEETING

This is another level up in terms of effort from the referral source who makes a personal phone call on your behalf and/or arranges a phone or in-person meeting between you and the prospect (in addition to many of the things outlined above). When your referral source arranges a call or a meeting between the two of you, that source moves beyond the role of a promoter and into the role of a connector or facilitator. This takes effort and is the sign of a committed referral partner who you should definitely support in return.

LEVEL 5: IN-PERSON INTRODUCTION AND PROMOTION

At this level, your referral source is making a serious commitment of time and energy in support of your business. She hasn't just arranged a meeting; she participates in the meeting. At this level, your referral source has done the work of assessing the need a prospect may have for your product or service and has gauged the prospect's interest in learning more about it. She shares this information with you, which enables you to tailor your products or services to emphasize the specific benefits that the prospect is looking for.

By agreeing to serve as an intermediary in a face-to-face introduction, your referral source becomes an active referral partner. This demonstration of deep trust in you and your product or service substantially raises the referral's effectiveness with the prospect.

This level is practically a "closed deal." Generally, a Level 5 referral means the business is nearly closed before you even contact the prospect, solely on the strength of your referral source's efforts. Not much is required from you except to answer some questions and deliver the product or service and collect the payment. People who give you Level 5 referrals are prized referral partners. Make sure to treat them as such. You should have a reciprocal relationship with these individuals. They are worth their weight in referral gold.

Figure 36.1 on page 257 contains a continuum that shows the amount of work you must do to close a prospect based on the level of the referral. If you're given a Level 1 referral, you have to do 95 percent of the work to close; this is not much better than other marketing efforts. On the other hand, if you get a Level 4 or 5 referral, then the person giving you the referral has already done most of the

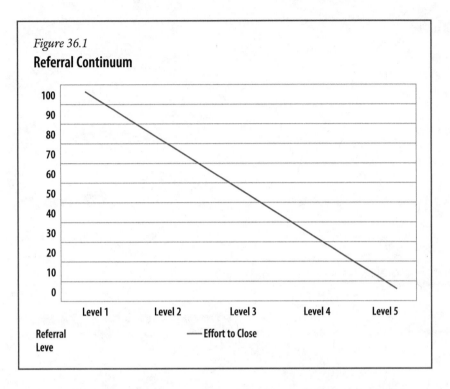

Figure 36.1
Referral Continuum

work for you. It's easier for your referral source to edify you than it is for you because your source already has a relationship of trust with your prospect. For this reason, it's important for you to do a superb job in fulfilling that referral, so your referrer will get great feedback and want to refer you again. The referral giver is, in essence, lending you his or her credibility; this is not something to be taken lightly.

Now that we've covered the five levels of referrals, let's proceed to the next chapter to look at the Networking Scorecard and see how we can track the work you're doing to develop your network.

37

The Networking Scorecard

Before you begin this chapter, note that we understand that copying this material or recreating it on an Excel spreadsheet can be a hassle, so we've created an app for the Networking Scorecard. Just go to www.IvanMisner.com/scorecard to download a copy.

It's a curious fact of human nature that many of us pay more attention to keeping track of our success at recreational activities than we do to tracking our success at the fundamentals of building our business. Avid golfers can tell you their handicap and recount almost shot for shot the last round they played. Bridge enthusiasts can talk for hours on strategy and exciting evenings at the card table. But how many of us who have a passion for a sport or hobby can give a detailed account of the things we did last week to strengthen our referral network?

The Networking Scorecard is a tool for keeping track of the things you do in the course of your week to build the effectiveness of your referral network. It lists a variety of activities that are proven strategies for enhancing relationships and assigns a point value to each one. Using the scorecard will remind you to do the things listed on it and will provide you with a valuable record of your networking activities and the results you can associate with them.

Sales managers around the world have continually looked for ways to measure the networking efforts of their sales forces. They want to go out and sell by networking, but most have failed to find measures of productivity they can feel confident using. The Networking Scorecard measures sales force activity in a number of ways; if the actions listed are accomplished and recorded, they can know that results will follow.

There are a number of things you can do to strengthen your relationships with your referral sources; the following tactics will build goodwill and credibility. Of course, this is not an exhaustive list, so feel free to add your own actions to it. Also, when we talk about "referral sources" in these descriptions, it can include "prospective" referral sources.

SEND A THANK-YOU CARD

Always a nice gesture, a handwritten thank-you card makes a great impression, especially in this age of electronic communication. Be sure to write a personalized note that mentions what you're thanking your referral source for. As we said before, www.SendOutCards.com is a great resource for this.

SEND A THANK-YOU GIFT

A gift is always welcome. Like a thank-you card, a gift, however small or inexpensive, builds visibility and credibility with your referral source. Try to find out what your referral source likes (favorite foods, hobbies, or other things), and then send a gift that is personalized to her tastes.

CALL A REFERRAL SOURCE

An occasional phone call is a good way to keep the relationship strong, if you take care to call only when it's least likely to be an unwelcome interruption. It's also a good idea to have a piece of news or some tidbit of information to pass along that will benefit or interest your source.

ARRANGE A ONE-TO-ONE MEETING

Meeting a referral source in person is an excellent opportunity to learn more about his business and interests. Prepare some questions in advance so that the conversation flows smoothly. Be ready to give an update on your business and to ask lots of questions about your source's interests.

ATTEND A NETWORKING EVENT

It's not called Net-sit or Net-eat, it's called NetWORK. You can't "Network Like a Pro" if you don't attend networking functions. Don't be a "cavedweller." Find the right streams of a network for you and get out there.

BRING SOMEONE WITH YOU TO THE NETWORKING EVENT

Invite a referral source to a networking event. Introducing her to other businesspeople you know gives your source an opportunity to meet others in your target market and may also provide new business opportunities. You become a connector to others. This is an important skill to develop.

SET UP AN ACTIVITY WITH MULTIPLE REFERRAL SOURCES

A recreational activity, such as a golf outing, fishing trip, concert, or play, is a great opportunity to let your referral source see a different side of you in an informal setting. The activity should be one that will give everybody time to relax, but it may also include an element of information, such as a speech or educational presentation. There really aren't any hard and fast "rules of engagement" during an informal, recreational event other than to have a good time, mix and mingle with everyone, and try not to "talk shop" too much. If you stick with that, everyone will likely have a good time.

GIVE A REFERRAL

Giving your referral source a referral is a wonderful way to build your relationship. By helping build your source's business, you create a debt of gratitude that will encourage your source to respond in kind. See Chapter 36 for the Five Levels of a Referral. Whenever possible, try to give level four or level five referrals.

SHARE OR SEND AN ARTICLE OF INTEREST

One of the great things about the information economy and today's internet world is that you always have access to good information.

So why not share different articles, blogs, or websites of interest to others in your network?

It doesn't cost you anything and if you're on Facebook, LinkedIn, or Twitter, it's super easy to hit that "share" button and let people know. Or you can do it individually with a personalized email. You can also go "old school" and set up a file for holding newspaper and magazine clippings that may be of interest to people you would like to be your referral sources. Regardless, sending an article, especially one that is pertinent to your source's current business or personal circumstances, says you are thinking about your source's needs.

ARRANGE A GROUP ACTIVITY FOR CLIENTS

Gathering your clients together creates an excellent environment for synergy and for raising your credibility with all. The one thing the people in this group will definitely have in common is you, so you'll certainly be the focus of a good many conversations. Group activities may be social, such as a barbecue or a ball game, or they may be educational, such as a seminar or a demonstration.

NOMINATE A REFERRAL SOURCE FOR RECOGNITION

Watch for opportunities to nominate a referral source for an award. Local service and civic organizations often present annual awards recognizing contributions to a particular cause, and local periodicals often sponsor award contests for businesspeople. Find out which groups and interests your referral source is involved in, and check to see if there is any form of recognition associated with them.

DISPLAY ANOTHER'S BROCHURE IN YOUR OFFICE

Doing a bit of sales work on behalf of a referral source can only enhance your relationship. If you have a public area for your business, offer to place your source's materials where your clients can read them.

INCLUDE OTHERS IN YOUR NEWSLETTER

Even a brief mention of a referral source in your newsletter can pay dividends down the road, including the opportunity for your source to reciprocate with his newsletter.

ARRANGE A SPEAKING ENGAGEMENT

Help your referral source get in front of a group that would be interested in her business or area of expertise. Local chapters of service organizations, such as Rotary and Kiwanis, are always looking for good speakers. If you belong to a group that invites people to speak, use your contacts to help your source make the rounds among various chapters. You can also apply this to yourself. When you have a chance to speak to a new group, it is a great opportunity to network.

POST TO SOCIAL MEDIA

Social media can be a good way to build your personal brand and stay connected with your referral sources and associates. Just remember not to get caught up in the black hole of funny cat videos. You're there to help build your network.

SHARE SOMETHING FROM SOMEONE ELSE VIA SOCIAL MEDIA

Engagement is key for your networking on social media. When you share people's appropriate content, you not only support them but you show others that you are active and engaged in the relationship process. Just remember the "black hole" rule. Don't get sucked into something that changes the space-time continuum for you where you lose all track of time and reduce your focus.

INVITE A SOURCE TO JOIN YOUR ADVISORY BOARD

Set up an informal board of advisors with whom you can meet regularly. Ask a referral source, who you feel could contribute valuable insights, to sit on your board. You can communicate with your board members via phone, email, newsletter, or occasional group meetings. Having an advisory board is important because people generally work best when they are accountable to someone other than themselves for accomplishing certain tasks. It's too easy to procrastinate when we have no one to answer to but ourselves. Whether you're starting a diet, beginning an exercise routine, or growing and developing your referral network, involving another person or group of people in the process will greatly enhance your chances for success.

Here's a riddle that illustrates the point of accountability: Five frogs sat on a log at the edge of a pond. Four of the frogs decided to jump into the pond. How many frogs were left sitting on the log? Answer: Five. Deciding to jump in and actually jumping are two different things.

Deciding to do the work of developing your network's effectiveness is only the first step in the process. You have to do it. The Networking Scorecard (see Figure 37.1 on page 26) is an excellent tool for holding yourself accountable for consistently doing the work that will enhance your network. We've added a couple "other" categories for you to add an activity that we didn't think of to measure your networking efforts. Just make sure that whatever you choose to add, is measurable and truly makes a difference to help you build a powerful personal network.

Figure 37.1
Networking Like a Pro Scorecard

Networking Like a Pro Weekly Score

Under 30 points	=	Apprentice
30–50 points	=	Intermediate
50–75 points	=	Advanced
75–100 points	=	Expert
100 or more	=	Master Networking Pro

Figure 37.1

Networking Like a Pro Scorecard, continued

Week of:								
Action	Points	Mon	Tue	Wed	Thurs	Fri	Total
Send a thank-you card	1×						
Send a thank-you gift	5×						
Call a referral source	2×						
Arrange a one-to-one	5×						
Attend a networking event	5×						
Bring someone with you to the networking event	5×						
Set up an activity with multiple referral sources	10×						
Give a referral (level of referral 4× = points)	___×						
Send an article of known interest to someone	5×						
Arrange a group activity for your clients	50×						
Nominate a referral source for recognition	10×						
Display another's brochures in your office (first time only)	10×						
Include others in your newsletter	5×						
Post to social media (maximum 1× per day)	1×						
Share something from someone else via social media (maximum 1× per day)	1×						
Arrange a speaking engagement for someone	10×						
Invite a source to join your advisory board (per person)	10×						
Other:	___×						
Other:	___×						
Total							

A

Credibility-
Enhancing
Materials Checklist

The following is a checklist of items you may already have available or wish to begin assembling, which can be used as collateral materials in developing your desired image.

You can store them physically with folders and hanging files if you'd like or digitally on your computer or in the cloud (this would include your website, testimonials, and things that are already online).

Just make sure it's stored in a place that's readily accessible and easy to find for both yourself and others.

CHECKLIST OF MATERIALS FOR DEVELOPING YOUR WORD-OF-MOUTH CAMPAIGN

❑ Testimonial letters from satisfied clients

❑ Photos of yourself and your office facilities, equipment, and products

❑ Photos of your key customers

❑ Photos of awards and certificates you and your staff have earned

❑ Articles in which you're mentioned

❑ Articles you have published

❑ A one-page flier you can scan

❑ Unpublished articles

❑ Audio or videos you have used

❑ Any of your new-product announcements or press releases that have been published

❑ Copies of other display advertisements that you've used (text from radio or TV spots)

❑ Advertisements that you've run

❑ A list of your memberships and affiliations

❑ Product catalogs you use

❑ Current brochures, circulars, and data sheets

❑ Question-and-answer sheets

❑ Logos, trademarks, service marks, patterns, and designs you've used

❑ Your letterhead and stationery

❑ Your annual report, capability statement, and prospectus

❑ Newsletters or news-type publications you use

❑ Your motto, mission statement, or service pledge

❑ Client or customer proposals and bid sheets

❑ Survey results by you or others

❑ Presentation notes or slides and PowerPoint presentations

❑ Marketing letters you wrote to clients

❑ Generic materials developed by your associations

❑ Articles on trends affecting your target market

❑ Posters, banners, and display materials used at trade shows

Note: This is not a complete list of items needed to market your business. The items in this list are focused on enhancing your networking activities.

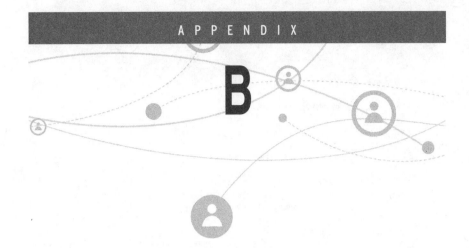

Do You Network Like a Pro?

I f you're not sure where to start when it comes to improving your networking results, then "rate your efforts" below, and that will go a long way toward figuring out where to focus your efforts.

Rate Your Efforts

Do you network like a pro?

1 = Never

3 = Sometimes

5 = Always

I have a referral plan and work the plan.	1	2	3	4	5
I track where all of my referrals come from.	1	2	3	4	5
I have a firm understanding of my target market.	1	2	3	4	5
I know the amount of business that I generate by referral.	1	2	3	4	5
I have a thank-you system for all of my referral sources.	1	2	3	4	5
I have an organized database system that is easy to use.	1	2	3	4	5
I keep my database updated regularly.	1	2	3	4	5
I have a mission statement for myself and my company.	1	2	3	4	5
I understand how to develop a referral partner.	1	2	3	4	5
I know the value of an appointment.	1	2	3	4	5
I have written goals for all of my networking groups.	1	2	3	4	5
I have a systematic approach for motivating my referral sources.	1	2	3	4	5
I have a system for staying in contact with my referral sources.	1	2	3	4	5
I know how many referrals I need to keep my pipeline full.	1	2	3	4	5
I know how to do focused networking.	1	2	3	4	5
I have a clear benefit statement for each of my products.	1	2	3	4	5
I understand the benefits of my products or services.	1	2	3	4	5
I have the ability to implement a new system in my business.	1	2	3	4	5
I understand the value of coaching and accountability partners.	1	2	3	4	5
I consistently get high-level referrals from my referral sources.	1	2	3	4	5
Total					

100	Networking like pro
80–99	A little tweaking needed
60–79	Some homework is necessary
40–59	Leads appear, but quite by accident
20–39	Lots of work needed, but it is a place to start

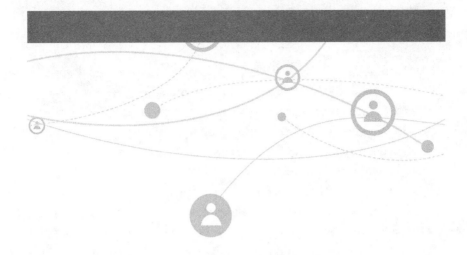

About the Authors

DR. IVAN MISNER is the founder and chief visionary officer of BNI, the world's largest business networking organization. BNI was founded in 1985. The organization now has over thousands of groups throughout every populated continent of the world. Each year, BNI generates millions of referrals resulting in billions of dollar's worth of business for its members.

Ivan's Ph.D. is from the University of Southern California. He has written 22 books, including his *New York Times* bestseller

Masters of Networking: Building Relationships for Your Pocketbook and Soul (Bard Press, 2000). He is a monthly columnist for Entrepreneur.com and is the senior partner for Asentiv, a referral training company with trainers around the world. In addition, he has taught business management and social capital courses at several universities throughout the United States.

Called the Father of Modern Networking by CNN and the Networking Guru by *Entrepreneur* magazine, Ivan is considered to be one of the world's leading experts on business networking and has been a keynote speaker for major corporations and associations throughout the world. He has been featured in the *Los Angeles Times*, *The Wall Street Journal*, and *The New York Times*, as well as numerous TV and radio shows on CNN, NBC, and the BBC in London.

Ivan spent almost two decades teaching at several universities and was also on the board of trustees for the University of La Verne. He is the cofounder of the BNI Charitable Foundation and was recently named Humanitarian of the Year by a Southern California newspaper. He is married and lives with his wife, Elisabeth, in Austin, Texas. In his spare time(!!!), he is also an amateur magician and a black belt in karate.

BRIAN HILLIARD is a popular speaker and author of the best-selling book *Networking Like a Pro!*

As creator of the program "How to Market Your Business in Less Than 90 Days," Brian works with busy entrepreneurs in the areas of marketing, mindset, and personal achievement.

Some of Brian's work has appeared nationally in *Black Enterprise*, *Coaching World* magazine, and the *Martha Zoller Morning Show*—where his interview was broadcast to over two million listeners.

Brian has also written the book *How to Overachieve without Overcommitting*, (Lightning Source/Ingram, 2006) and since 2001 has engaged literally thousands of people through his speaking and coaching programs.

Prior to starting his own business, Brian earned his degree at Duke University in the areas of marketing and economics.

During his free time, Brian enjoys playing golf and basketball and watching as many movies as humanly possible!

 ASENTIV is a leading referral training organization, with franchises, trainers, and coaches around the world. The organization teaches business professionals how to harness the power of referral marketing to drive sales for long-term, sustainable business growth by referral.

The organization offers students one-day programs as well as courses covering several modules over 10 to 12 weeks. The Pipeline Program, the organization's signature class, requires participants to attend the class with a referral source. The one-day Pipeline Seminar teaches a simple, highly manageable referral process by which participants leave the training having already scheduled appointments with qualified prospects.

The Referral Institute's 10- to 12-week course is called Certified Networker®. This course is truly a foundation for understanding, developing, and tracking your referral business. In most cases, Certified Networker simply changes the way business owners do business. It narrows their target market, provides them with mission statements, and shows them how profitable it can be to develop referral sources by being strategic. Certified Networker is a must for anyone new to referral marketing.

Please go to www.Asentiv.com to learn more about referral marketing as well as how to attend a training program in your area.

BNI® BNI, the world's largest business networking organization, was founded by Dr. Ivan Misner in 1985 as a way for businesspeople to generate referrals in a structured, professional environment. The organization, now the world's largest referral business network, has thousands of chapters with tens of thousands of members on every populated continent. Since the organization's inception, BNI members have passed millions of referrals, generating billions of dollars in business for the participants.

The primary purpose of the organization is to pass qualified business referrals to its members. The philosophy of BNI can be summed up in two simple words: Givers Gain®. If you give business to people, you will get business from them. BNI allows only one person per profession to join a chapter. The program is designed to help businesspeople develop long-term relationships, thereby creating a basis for trust and, inevitably, referrals. The mission of BNI is to help members increase their business through a structured, positive, and professional word-of-mouth program that enables them to develop long-term, meaningful relationships with quality business professionals.

To visit a chapter near you, visit its website at www.bni.com.

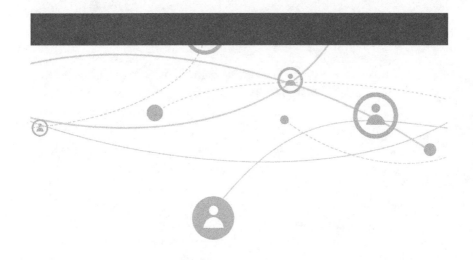

Index

A

abundance mindset, 30–34,
    51–52. *See also* Givers Gain
*Achieving Success Through Social
    Capital* (Baker), 24
advisory boards, 263–264
alumni networks, 42
ambassadors at events, 8, 9
appearance, 131
article sharing with referral
    sources, 262
Asentiv training programs, 275
asking for referrals, 207–208

asking for the sale, 108
asking how you can help, 245–
    247. *See also* Givers Gain
asking questions showing
    interest in others, 21, 34, 37,
    57–58
attention focus, 145–148
attitude, 131

B

behavioral styles in networking,
    117–121
benefits of networking, 3–4
blogging, 92–93

BNI (Business Network International), 9, 25, 67–69, 276
body language, 131
brand building with social media, 87–88
Branson, Richard, 46–47
broadening your network, 56, 76
business cards at networking events, 132–133
business networking organizations. *See* networking organizations
business school curriculum, 15–17
butterfly effect, 45–48

C
calling past clients, 177–178
calling referral sources, 261
Canfield, Jack, 46
casual-contact networks, 65–67
chambers of commerce, 66–67
chance nature of networking, 49–52
choosing networking groups, 76–77
client activities, 262
client appreciation events, 175–177
closed configuration, 125–127
CMS (contact management system), 209–213
coffee connections, 6, 205–208, 210. *See also* one-to-one meetings
cold calling, 113–114
college curriculum, 15–17

community service clubs, 69–72
company story, 155–161
competitors, referring business to, 32–34
complementary businesses, 33, 174–175
confidence, referral, 81, 191–196
connecting over nonbusiness interests, 59
connections, 56
connectors, 42
contact management system (CMS), 209–213
contacts, 56
contacts, referring, 38–39
contacts vs. relationships, 27. *See also* relationship building
Contactually, 213
credibility, 63, 64, 143, 262
credibility-enhancing material checklist, 267–269
customer relationship manager (CRM), 209–213
customer-based word-of-mouth, 7
customers as referral sources, 7

D
databases, contact, 209–213
direct referrals, 38
directness, 108
disconnect in networking, 19–22
discounts, 235–236
displaying referral source's brochures, 263
diversifying your network, 21, 41–44, 76–77

E

elevator pitches, 134–135

email signatures, 178–179

enewsletters, 93

events. *See* networking events

events, non-networking, 243–247

Examiners, 120–121

expert status, 215–221

extroverts, 7–10, 110

F

Facebook, 75, 88–90

face-to-face networking

behavioral styles, 117–121

characteristics of great networkers, 103–106

cold calling approach to, 113–114

common networking mistakes, 111–116

least important skills for networking, 107–110

online networking vs., 81–85

where to start at an event, 123–128

farming vs. hunting, 35–40, 49–50, 76, 104–106

fearlessness, 108

finder's fees, 234

first 12 words out of your mouth, 133–134

focused attention, 145–148

follow-up, 6, 22, 112, 199, 201–203. *See also* coffee connections; one-to-one meetings

formalized referral strategies, 173–179

G

GAINS profile, 58–59

gatekeepers, referral, 52, 225–231

George, Kim, 46

Givers Gain, 25–26, 29–30, 34, 71, 245–247. *See also* reciprocity

giving away business, 30–34, 51–52. *See also* Givers Gain

Go-Getters, 118–119

good referrals, symptoms of, 187–190

group activities for clients, 262

group dynamics, 123–128

H

heterogeneous networks, 21, 41–44, 76–77

Hilliard, Brian, 274–275

hub firms, 230–231

hunting for prospects, 35–36. *See also* farming vs. hunting

I

incentive triangulation, 236–237

incentives for referrals, 234–241

in-person introduction and promotion, 256

interviewing skills, 21

introductory calls, 255–256

introverts, 7–10, 110

inviting referral sources to events, 261

inviting referral sources to join your advisory board, 263–264

isolation, working in, 26

K

Knowledge and Social Capital (Lesser), 25

knowledgeable experts, 215–221

L

law of reciprocity, 29–34, 51–52

Less Annoying CRM, 212

leveraging new contacts, 197–208

linchpins, 42

listening skills, 145–148

M

measuring networking success, 5–6. *See also* networking like a pro rating sheet; Networking Scorecard

meetings with prospects, 255–256

membership composition in networking groups, 4–5

Misner, Ivan, 273–274

mistakes, networking, 111–116

mixer group dynamics, 124–128

N

name and contact information, 254–255

networking at non-networking events, 243–247

networking benefits, 3–4, 5

networking disconnect, 19–22

networking events. *See also* non-networking events

determining the right event, 137–144

group dynamics at, 123–128

maximizing event strategy, 168–170

quality vs. quantity at, 163–170

relationship building at, 165–167

standing out at, 149–154

12 x 12 x 12 Rule and, 129–135

visitor hosting at, 8, 9

networking face-to-face. *See* face-to-face networking

networking like a pro rating sheet, 271–272. *See also* Networking Scorecard

networking online. *See* online networking

networking organizations

building social capital in, 25–27

casual-contact networks, 65–67

choosing, 76–77

community service clubs, 69–72

professional associations, 73–74

rise of, 25

social media networks, 74–76

strong-contact networks, 25, 67–69

networking partners, 7, 48, 114–115, 194. *See also* referral partners

Networking Scorecard, 259–266. *See also* networking like a pro rating sheet networking success, measuring, 5–6. *See also* networking like a pro rating sheet; Networking Scorecard

networking vs. cold calling, 113–114

newsletter mentions of referral sources, 263

newsletters, online, 93

nominating referral sources for awards, 263

nonbusiness interests, connecting over, 59

non-networking events, 243–247

nontraditional settings for networking, 243–244

Nurturers, 119–120

O

offering free advice, 37–38

one-to-one meetings, 6, 22, 199, 202–203, 261. *See also* coffee connections

online communications, 92–93

online marketing, 75, 88

online networking
    blogging, 92–93
    brand building with, 87–88
    enewsletters as, 93
    face-to-face networking vs., 81–85
    future of, 89–90
    integrating with face-to-face networking, 87
    pros and cons, 79–81, 85–89
    social capital and, 92

social media networks, 74–76

strategy for, 75–76, 88–89, 91–92, 93

VCP Process and, 81, 93

online newsletters, 93, 174

open configuration, 126, 127

P

power teams, 33, 174–175

professional associations, 73–74

profitability, 63–64, 143

Promoters, 119

promoting your business through others, 249–252, 256–257

P.S. messages in email signatures, 178–179

purpose of networking, 20

Q

questions, standout, 149–154

R

rating your networking efforts, 271–272. *See also* Networking Scorecard

reciprocity, 29–34, 51–52. *See also* Givers Gain

recreational activities with referral sources, 261–262

referral confidence, 81, 191–196

referral continuum, 256–257

referral gatekeepers, 52, 225–231

referral groups, 25, 67–69

Referral Institute course, 275

referral levels, 253–257

referral networking, 5–6, 11

referral partners, 21, 36, 56–58, 114–115, 130, 233–241, 260–261. *See also* networking partners

referral strategies, formalized, 173–179

referrals, symptoms of good, 188–190

referring business to others, 30, 31–34, 51–52

referring contacts, 38–39

referring your referral sources, 262

relationship building, 3–4, 20–21, 27–28, 55–59, 76, 165–167. *See also* VCP Process

relationship networking. *See also* Givers Gain

   farming vs. hunting, 35–40, 49–50, 76, 104–106

   reciprocity in, 29–34, 51–52

reputation of referrer, 193–194

responsiveness to referral partners, 114–115

rewarding referral partners, 234–241

risk to reputation, 193–194

ROI (return on investment), 24, 76

Rotary International, 70

Rutan, Burt, 47

S

Salzman, Nancy, 46

searchlight networkers, 147

self-promotion, 108

selling at networking events, 19–20, 35–36. *See also* farming vs. hunting

SendOutCards.com, 202

sharing personal experience, 255

sincerity, 247

situational extroverts, 9

social capital, 23–28, 71–72, 92, 181–185

social events, networking at, 243–247

social media networks, 74–76, 88–90, 91. *See also* online networking

social media savviness, 108–109

speaking engagements for referral sources, 263

spheres of influence, 96–99

standing out at networking events, 149–154

strategies for success

   diversification, 21, 41–44, 76–77

   event strategies, 168–170

   formalized referral strategies, 173–179

   online networking strategies, 75–77, 88–89, 91–92, 93

   relationship building, 55–59

strong-contact networks, 25, 67–69

supplementary material, 255

systematic referral marketing, 250–252

T

target markets, 95–99, 138–139

thanking referral partners, 233–241, 260–261
thank-you cards and gifts, 260
time investment in others, 194–195
tracking networking activities, 6
transactions vs. relationships, 30
trigger point approach, 190
trust, 25–26, 59, 62
12 x 12 x 12 Rule, 129–135

U

unique selling proposition (USP), 112–113, 133, 134, 156–159

V

VCP Process, 61–64, 81, 93, 143. *See also* relationship building
videoconferencing, 82
Vipor Plus, 212
visibility, 62–63, 64, 143, 187–188
visitor hosting at events, 8, 9
volunteering, 8, 26–27, 43–44, 66, 74

W

word-of-mouth marketing, 7, 118, 156, 187–190, 268–269

Network on the Go with
the Networking Scorecard™ App

I n business, you achieve what you measure. Now, you can take all of the *Networking Like a Pro* action items with you on the go. The Networking Scorecard™ App provides you with a mobile solution to measuring your networking efforts so you can:

- Track networking activities like thank-you notes, meetings, calls, events, and referrals

- Earn points to track your networking skill level and performance

- View weekly networking activities at-a-glance

- Set up a customized networking calendar

- Access resources from Dr. Ivan Misner, Brian Hilliard, BNI, and Asentiv

- And most importantly, measure if you are Networking Like a Pro!

Go to www.IvanMisner.com/Scorecard
to download the app now